MOTHER OF THAT WISDOM

OTHER PLAYS BY JOSEPH KESSELRING

Aggie Appleby, Maker of Men (1933)
There's Wisdom in Women (1935)
Cross-Town (1937)
Arsenic and Old Lace (1941)
Maggie McGilligan (1942)
Identically Yours (1945)
4 Twelves Are 48 (1949)
Surgery Is Indicated (1954)
Accidental Angel (1955)
A Frog in His Pocket (1958)
Bearded Lady with a Kindly Knife (1964)

Mother of That Wisdom

A historical play in two acts by
Joseph Kesselring

An Exposition-Banner Book

Exposition Press   New York

EXPOSITION PRESS, INC.
50 Jericho Turnpike, Jericho, New York 11753

CHARACTERS
(in order of appearance)

HETH, a Hittite ⎫
MEMUCAN, a Hittite ⎬ mercenaries
BICHRI, an Edomite ⎭

ISHUI ⎫
HOSAH ⎬ Jewish soldiers

ABISHAG, handmaiden to Bath-sheba, concubine of Solomon
HATHOP, an arrogant Egyptian
REHOBOAM, the prince
SERVANT to Rehoboam
JEROBOAM
TIKVAH, a court idler
AZARIAH, Captain of the City Host
BENAIAH, Captain of the Host of Israel
ZADOK, the chief priest
AD'HOTEP, a noble Egyptian
ITTAI, a young lutist
AHISHER, the Palace Prefect
TAHPNES, Egyptian wife of Solomon, daughter of the pharaoh
NAAMAH, mother of the prince
SOLOMON, king of Israel
KINYRAS, an elderly Phoenician, Mariner of Tyre
BATH-SHEBA, Queen-mother
ZABUD, the Grand Prefect of Israel

vii

MAN A

MAN B

WOMAN B ⎫

WOMAN A ⎭ who claim the same child

ADONIRAM, Overseer of Public Works

AHURAM, the Tyrian emissary of King Hiram

GIRL A, one of Solomon's concubines

MAACAH, mother of Absalom (son of David)

MALE SERVANT to Bath-sheba

DWARF A

SERVANT to Tahpnes

GIRL 1 ⎫

GIRL 2 ⎬ three of Solomon's concubines, each pregnant

GIRL 3 ⎭

LITTLE BOO, a young harlot

FOLLOWER 1 ⎫

FOLLOWER 2   friends of Jeroboam

FOLLOWER 3 ⎭

OLD MAN of Gad, the charcoal burner, also referred to as GADITE

NAPHTALITE ⎫

ZEBULONITE ⎪

ISSACHARITE ⎬ FOUR GALILEANS

ASHERITE ⎭

SIMEONITE

SERVANT to Bath-sheba

IDLER A

IDLER B

IDLER C

IDLER D

NABOTH, a wounded priest

SECOND PRIEST

THIRD PRIEST
BOZ, Captain of the Palace Guard
SERVANT to Solomon
GUARD CAPTAIN
MESSENGER of Zadok
SHIMEI, Captain of the Southern Host

Also four Caucasian slaves; three black slaves; Nubian mutes (at least four); two young student rabbis; two white Egyptian mutes (AD'HOTEP's slaves); cosmopolitan dandies, wealthy merchants, city officials, wives, mothers, armored captains; an orchestra of six musicians; four Egyptian priests; Jehoshaphat, the Recorder; Elihoreph and Ahiah, Scribes, two attendants to BATH-SHEBA; six giggling girls; two trumpeters; a dwarf; four joyous revelers; palace officials; attendants to SOLOMON.

AUTHOR'S NOTE

The character names in the play are historical. Due to the unfamiliarity of most of them to the modern mind and eye—and to occasional similarity, one to the other —they may seem confusing to the casual reader. Character and costume differences, however, will simplify identification in performance of the play.

TIME AND PLACE   The year is 965 B.C., Jerusalem, in ancient Israel, during the fifth year of the reign of King Solomon.

ACT ONE

ACT ONE

Scene I

SCENE   *The Porch of Judgment in the palace of Solo-*
mon. It is part of the Porch of Pillars on the palace front.
The scene proper is a sunken pavilion backed by marble
pillars set into a marble railing. The top of the railing
is 8 feet above the stage floor, its base 4 feet above the
floor. Along this base runs a narrow Guards' Walk of
cedar wood. The railing, which runs circularly across the
back of the stage, is widely broken in the center creating
a portal. Some 8 shallow steps lead up to this portal from
the pavilion floor. The portal leads out to the Place of
Judgment, which is a marble terrace, some 8 feet by 12,
that looks down on the 50 marble steps of the palace and
at their foot, on the Judgment Square.

The complete set is so angled that stage R has con-
siderably greater depth than L. This gives an off-center
angle to the Place of Judgment (terrace C), so that, to
stand on it, facing directly away from the set, would be
to face U by L, rather than directly U.

The cedar floor of the pavilion is spread with rugs.
Large cedar beams decorate a painted blue ceiling.
Heavy draw-curtains of red-and-white-striped silk hang
between the pillars. The curtains, drawn, serve to screen
out heat and noise and convert the pavilion into an in-

3

timate assembly chamber. Additional storm curtains of heavy tan wool are rolled to the pillar tops outside the silken draperies. Rich furniture of the period is scattered around. There are chairs and low tables and many cushions. UL there is a chair quite large and ornate; elevated, it might be a low-backed throne. L of C and somewhat U is an ornate divan. Beside it, R, is a smaller divan, also pretentious.

At Rise   *It is early afternoon. The low off-stage noise of a gathering multitude on the Judgment Square is heard through the drawn silken curtains.*

Positioned on the steps and the Guards' Walk, five palace guards stand in military stiffness. They are costumed in the gleaming bronze armor and helmet of the army of ancient Israel, the helmet carrying the white plume of the Jerusalem Host. A short skirt, sandals and bronze shin guards complete the costume. In addition to a round shield, a sword and a spear, each is armed with a triple-lashed whip that hangs coiled at his sword belt.

Two of the soldiers, ISHUI *and* HOSAH, *are young, light-bearded Jews. The remaining three are Semite mercenaries, heavily bearded men in their thirties:* BICHRI, *an Edomite, and* HETH *and* MEMUCAN, *Hittites.*

An elderly servant, white-robed, gray-bearded, directs three Caucasian slaves. They elevate the larger of the two divans by setting it on a low platform, arrange furniture (chairs and tables) around the two divans. Three black slaves bring in bowls of fruit, jugs of wine and cups, place them on tables, directed by second servant.

MOTHER OF THAT WISDOM

With the exit of the servants and slaves, L, the three mer-cenaries relax cautiously. They indicate that the heat is great and their armor uncomfortable.
The two Jewish soldiers remain motionless.
The noise of the multitude swells momentarily.

HETH
(Ascends the steps, pulls aside a curtain,
looks out over the multitude)
Baal's bowels! Thousands of them! Packed like figs in a jar! *(Snapping curtain shut.)*

MEMUCAN
And the temple workers still to come. *(Helping him-self to grapes)* Dolts!

BICHRI
Idiots! Jewish idiots! *(Easing himself down to sit on a step)* Trample each other like sheep to watch Solomon play God.

MEMUCAN
Not "God," my dear fellow heathen. "Jehovah!" *(To the two Jews who still stand stiffly motionless)* Eh, Israel?

BICHRI
Up yours, soldier. *(Wiping his face with a cloth)* God is a God is a Jewish Jehovah. *(Blows a soft "bird.")*

5

HETH

Such vulgarity. (*Taking grapes*) Anyway, the mob's not here today for Solomon, they want to see the freaks from the ships.

MEMUCAN

That's right, I hear they've got little naked men, covered with hair.

HETH

Yeah, black. And teeth this long, they say (*indicating four feet*). Aps, they call them.

BICHRI

Apes, stupid. (*Wiping himself under his breastplate*) Send ships sailing around for three years and come back with freaks. Where's the gold?

HETH

I heard they had freak birds, too. Pea birds.

BICHRI

Wonderful. They'll give us our back pay in pea birds. (*He stretches, groans*) Baal, but my loins ache.

MEMUCAN

Too much wall climbing?

BICHRI

Ha!

MOTHER OF THAT WISDOM

HETH
(*To* MEMUCAN)
The men of Edom seem to be weak below the waist.

BICHRI
If you jelly-bellied Hittites had had my night in the
king's private pasture, you'd be so weak you'd—

(MEMUCAN *silences him, warningly indicating the
two young Jews.*)

HETH
(*He approaches the rigid* HOSAH)
Have a grape (*holding a grape to* HOSAH'S *mouth*).

HOSAH
(*Twisting his head*)
Go away!

HETH
He's alive! (*Moves to* ISHUI *and jams a grape against
his mouth*) Have a grape, Israel.

ISHUI
Stop that, you damned mercenary!

HETH
What, good Jewish grapes?

MEMUCAN
Relax, Israel, relax. (*Chooses a cake.*)

7

ISHUI

You'll relax, you stupid doll worshiper, if the captain Azariah catches you!

HETH

(As MEMUCAN *blows a "bird")*
Azariah! Ha! Another boy soldier.

HOSAH

I suppose he got that scar by picking his nose!

HETH

Anybody can get a scar.

MEMUCAN

You just let somebody cut you. Speaking of cutting, I hear Benaiah's in the city.

ISHUI

The *lord* Benaiah?

MEMUCAN

Captain of the Host of Israel—and no boy.

BICHRI

And *that's* the truth! Did I ever tell you how he slew those Moabites?

HETH and MEMUCAN

Yes!

8

HOSAH

Were you there?

BICHRI

Was I there, of *course* I was there! What a sight! (*He acts it out.* HOSAH *and* ISHUI *are drawn from their posts*) Here they are, you see, four of them, behind this rock, big as lions and armed. And here's Benaiah with his bare hands. He crouches. Then he walks, just *walks* around that rock—like a cat. Then it's one! two! three! *four*— and there they are, *all* of them, dead as leather And him not even winded! What a Jew!

ISHUI

By Jehovah!

HOSAH

A hero! A true hero!

(BICHRI *hisses suddenly and leaps to his post.* HETH *and* MEMUCAN *follow on the jump.* HOSAH *and* ISHUI *are left off post as* ABISHAG *enters L. She is 21 years old, darkly beautiful. Though slender, she is lushly developed. The men freeze, think better of it, move stiffly to their posts. Three servants follow* ABISHAG. *They bear six small stools, cushions and a large woolen shawl.*)

ABISHAG

Move this over—close———right against. (*The ser-*

vants move a chair close to the left of the large divan)
Right *against!* ... Now group the stools here, around the
queen-mother's chair. ... Not *too* close, she doesn't want
the girls in her *lap!* (*The servants obey*) There. Now a
cushion on each stool. (*The servants obey.* ABISHAG
*throws the shawl over the chair, pads the chair with
cushions.*)

(HATHOP *enters L followed by four Nubian mutes.*
HATHOP *is an arrogant Egyptian, smooth-shaven,
clad in the costume of his native land. At his waist
is a coiled Egyptian whip, the tips of its three lashes
laced with lead. Apart from loin skirt and headdress
the Nubian mutes are naked. They bear an array of
Egyptian comforts: padded silken coverings for the
small divan and the floor, cushions, bottles of lo-
tions, trays of dainties to be nibbled, a large fan of
feathers. By the snapping of his fingers* HATHOP
*directs the arranging of the comforts on and around
the small divan.* ABISHAG *watches warily. A mute
tips over a bottle.*)

HATHOP

Careful, fool! (*With a threatening hand to his whip.
A second mute, by throat sounds, asks directions for the
place of floor cushions*) Here and around to the left.

ABISHAG

Oh, no! The queen-mother's people won't be able to
see the treasure!

MOTHER OF THAT WISDOM

HATHOP
(Eyeing her insolently)
You are that Abishag?—the king's concubine?

ABISHAG
I am also *that Abishag,* handmaiden to the queen-mother—whose people come first!

HATHOP
The Queen Tahpnes sits on the king's right hand! (*Indicating divans*) Therefore her people come first!

ABISHAG
If such things delight her she can sit on his right foot! This is Israel! The Egyptian woman comes second to the lady Bath-sheba! (*She kicks the Egyptian cushions R.*)

HATHOP
Hebrew scum!

(Exits, the mutes follow.)

ABISHAG
Nasty heathen! (*She kicks a cushion*) The lady Bath-sheba should have another shawl on her chair. And a foot stool and some of those honey cakes she likes. Come!

(She exits. The servants follow her.)

BICHRI
Moloch's bones! (*Leering libidinously*) And they say she's never even been bounced!

11

MOTHER OF THAT WISDOM

HOSAH

Keep your dirty tongue off her! She's a decent girl!

BICHRI

That's what I said. (*Moving D*) It's a shame.

MEMUCAN

Old-fashioned tragedy. (*Moving D.*)

HETH

(*He has moved D. Strokes the cover on Queen
Tahpnes' divan*)

Know what I heard about this one? You know that
big Syrian?—the cockeyed one? He was on duty outside
her pavilion. She called him in and— (*He sticks out his
lower lip and nods.* BICHRI, *who is sampling wine, blows
a "bird"*) All right, he told me himself.

ISHUI

You mean the *queen?*

HOSAH

The *Queen Tahpnes?*

HETH

Why not? What's a crown? Just another thing she
has to take off.

(BICHRI *hisses, jumps to his post.* HETH *and* MEMU-
CAN *follow.*

HOSAH *and* ISHUI *again are caught off post, freezing.*

REHOBOAM *enters L. A handsome blond youngster of 7. He is riding a toy pole-horse atop a small divan borne on the shoulders of four Caucasian slaves. A* SERVANT *follows.)*

REHOBOAM
(He whips the divan with a small whip)
Forward! Attack!

SERVANT
(To HOSAH *and* ISHUI *who block the way)*
Passage for the Prince Rehoboam!

REHOBOAM
Make way, you idiots! . . . *(The two Jewish guards move to their posts)* Forward! *Go!* . . . *(The slaves trot)* All right, put it down! Stop! Put it *down!* . . . *(The slaves lower the divan,* REHOBOAM *jumps off)* Put it here! Hold my horse, you fool! (SERVANT *props the horse against a table. Slaves set the divan beside that of the queen Tahpnes)* Closer, right up against. . . . Now the things, this one on the floor.

(Silken coverings and cushions are spread about.)

SERVANT
If the king's son will permit: your divan is resting on the queen Tahpnes' floor covering.

13

REHOBOAM

She told me to put it close. (*To slave*) Not there, you idiot, for the cushion! The top! The *top!* (*The slave backs, knocks over the toy horse*) You clumsy dog! Come here! (*Cringing, the slave obeys.* REHOBOAM *looks at his small whip, tosses it away*) You! (*To* BICHRI) Give me your whip!

(BICHRI *hands over his whip.*

JEROBOAM *enters R. He is 27 years old, slender and sleek, smooth of gesture and tongue. The fingers of his pale hands are heavily ringed, his black beard shines with oil. In his dress he strives for magnificence.* TIKVAH, *a court idler, follows him. They stand unobserved.*)

SERVANT

But my lord, a poor slave!—

REHOBOAM

Silence! (*To slave*) Bend over! (*The slave obeys.* REHOBOAM *raises the whip, tenses—but finds himself slightly sick. He thrusts the whip at* BICHRI) Whip him! (BICHRI *takes the whip, raises it.* REHOBOAM *averts his face. Observing this,* BICHRI *lashes the divan. The slave turns his head in surprise, then cries out. Again* BICHRI *lashes the divan, again the slave cries out*) There! Wait! Enough! Let that be a lesson to you! To all of you! Yes! My father whips you, then *I* can whip you! And I'll whip harder!—

14

MOTHER OF THAT WISDOM

JEROBOAM

*(He has crossed, bends a knee—*TIKVAH *following,
aping)*

My lord the Prince Rehoboam!

REHOBOAM

Jeroboam! I was just whipping this slave.

JEROBOAM

(Sneering frankly)

So I observed, my lord.

TIKVAH

(Clumsily false)

You did give it to him good, didn't you, my lord!

REHOBOAM

(Eyeing the idler haughtily)

Some day I shall whip men who are *not* slaves. (*To*
SERVANT) My horse! (*He mounts the pole-horse*) Forward! *Go!* (*He gallops around the stage*) *Attack!* (*He
gallops off L. Servants and slaves follow.*)

JEROBOAM

*(Sneers audibly, pours himself a large cup of wine,
tosses it off, pours another. With a gesture he gives
his creature,* TIKVAH, *permission to drink)*

An Egyptian wine. More exciting than ours.

TIKVAH

Thank you, my lord! (*He pours eagerly. He is a*

*short, round buffoon who lives but to tipple and ape his
seeming betters.*)

JEROBOAM

You see what is in store for you, my good Tikvah,
when the cub wears the crown.

TIKVAH

"When," my lord, eh?—"when."

JEROBOAM

Softly. (*He crosses to* BICHRI, *stares at him*) Your
name?

BICHRI

Bichri of Edom, my lord.

JEROBOAM

You know who I am?

BICHRI

Jeroboam, Lord of the Labor Drafts, my lord.

JEROBOAM

Yes. . . . You disobeyed the prince. I could break
you, put you to work in the mines of Arabah. You would
soon die. . . . Remember that I did nothing of the kind.
(*He returns D, drinks another cup of wine, wipes his lips,
exits L.* TIKVAH *gulps a last drink and follows.*)

16

MOTHER OF THAT WISDOM

BICHRI

Slimy bastard!

HETH

By Moloch!—a nasty potful that one, uh?

BICHRI

Vulture vomit!

MEMUCAN

And that little prince of pus pockets! (*To* HOSAH *and* ISHUI) A lovely king you Jews are going to have!

ISHUI

The boy is all right at heart. He could not even watch the punishment. He's spoiled, that's all.

MEMUCAN

Till he stinks!

(The noise of the multitude suddenly swells.)

HETH
(Ascends steps, peers between curtains)
It's that big mangy priest again.

ISHUI

Ahijah?

HETH

Ahijah. (*Laughing*) *He* should be king. They're squatting all around him like dogs.

17

MOTHER OF THAT WISDOM

ISHUI

(He has ascended steps, peers out)

It is he, the Shilonite!

HETH

(Descending steps)

Crazy as a Greek.

HOSAH

(As he ascends to see)

You ignorant fool! He's a man of God, a prophet!

HETH

Where I come from we keep them in pits.

MEMUCAN

The Jews and their prophets. Who cares what's going to happen? If it does, you can't stop it. If it doesn't, then it was a lie in the first place.

BICHRI

I don't know. That fellow Nathan had something. David was no gull for crackpots, and neither was Bath-sheba—which she *still* isn't, *rumor* to the *contrary*. And old Nathan was sort of private prophet to the family. And he could do his job, too. I remember about ten years ago: Old Captain Joab was getting a bit biggity about *his* host, *his* soldiers, and Nathan stuck his finger at old Joab's Adam's apple and he said—right in front of *me* he said it! —he said: "The unholy pride of Joab is the sword that will pierce his throat!" And you know what happened to old Joab.

18

MEMUCAN

By Baal! And that's where he *got* it?

BICHRI

Right.

HETH

And *Benaiah* gave it to him!

BICHRI

Correct. *Our* Captain Benaiah. Not that I'm compar-ing Nathan with *that* scurvy old lunatic that should be —*P'ssst!*

(He leaps for his post. HETH *and* MEMUCAN *also leap.*

HOSAH *and* ISHUI, *heads thrust absorbedly through the curtains, remain off post.*

BENAIAH *and* AZARIAH *enter R.*

BENAIAH *is one of the remarkable characters of his age and looks the part. A man of 50, he is 200 pounds of tall, craggy strength. His black beard is shot with gray. As Captain of the Host of Israel his armor is of gold; his gold helmet bears a plume combining the colors of the three hosts: red for Northern, blue for Southern and white for City. He is armed with a sword but carries no whip.*

19

MOTHER OF THAT WISDOM

AZARIAH, *Captain of the City (Jerusalem) Host, is a
large brown-bearded man of 30. He is likable but
lacking in brilliance. He affects a ponderous frown.
A livid scar marks his right cheek from temple to
mouth. Befitting his rank his armor is plated with
gold; his golden helmet holds the white plume of
the City Host. He wears a sword. A whip is tucked
into his belt.)*

AZARIAH
(He halts at sight of HOSAH *and* ISHUI *at the curtains,
draws his whip, snaps it at their bottoms)*
To your posts! (HOSAH *and* ISHUI *obey on the jump)*
Report yourselves for lashes! Ten! Er—five!

HOSAH
If the Captain Azariah will permit—the multitude
seemed—

AZARIAH
Silence! (*To* BENAIAH) My lord, I am ashamed.

BENAIAH
(Regarding the five guards)
Very pretty. They look just like soldiers. (*He takes
a cake from the hand of* MEMUCAN) Cakes. On duty.
(*Eyeing* BICHRI—*while munching the cake*) Bichri, of
Edom.

BICHRI
(Going to one knee)
My lord Benaiah!

BENAIAH

Get up, you old wench hound. (*To all of them*)
What are you guarding here?

HETH

The palace, my lord!

BICHRI

The *king,* my lord!

BENAIAH

Guard *it* and *him* some place else. Get out.

AZARIAH

Smartly now. Hup! (*The five guards exit R*) Inexcusable!

BENAIAH

You see what I mean? The dry rot of inactivity, of
peace. The entire host is eaten with it. In fact, Israel, all
of it. . . . David should see his Israel—soft—effeminate.

AZARIAH

But my lord, there's constant fighting. The borders:
there's never a week that—

BENAIAH

Yes, yes, we maintain the peace! But we do *not* wage
war! If you can't see the difference you belong in some
other business.

AZARIAH

Well, of course I see the difference, my lord. But I did think that anything—

BENAIAH

You *don't* think! Not like a soldier! It is your misfortune, not your fault. War makes the soldier and Israel is ruled by a love-sick pacifist. So you will remain just what you are: a pleasant young man who happens to be the son of Zadok, Chief Priest of Israel.

AZARIAH

(Touching his scar)

There was the engagement at Damascus. I had five hundred against thousands and I triumphed.

BENAIAH

Five hundred trained men and fifty chariots—against a disorganized rabble. (AZARIAH *lowers his head*) I am sorry, lad. You did well. (*Then a shade more casually*) Well enough that it galls me to see you blocked by— circumstance. You might have developed into a hero. (*He studies a dish of cakes.*)

AZARIAH

But what can one do, my lord?

BENAIAH

Well—(*Selecting a cake*) perhaps it is a matter of loyalty.

22

MOTHER OF THAT WISDOM

AZARIAH

Loyalty?

BENAIAH

To whom do you owe your first loyalty, Azariah?

AZARIAH

To the king.

BENAIAH

Not to Israel?

AZARIAH

But—the king *is* Israel.

BENAIAH

The crown is Israel, the king is a man. Would you destroy Israel at the bidding of a man?

AZARIAH

Why—no! No, of course not!

BENAIAH

Neither would I, lad. We are soldiers, you and I— of Israel. And *for* Israel. Let us remember that.

(ZADOK, *the chief priest, enters followed by two young student rabbis who attend him. He is a noble son of Israel and a true Holy Man. The cares of his office have bowed his shoulders and whitened his beard. He wears the robes and headdress of his office. He walks with a staff of office.)*

MOTHER OF THAT WISDOM

ZADOK

Benaiah, my dear old friend!

BENAIAH

(As they embrace.)
Zadok, old rabbi, it's good to see you again!

ZADOK

It must be almost a year.

BENAIAH

I have been working. Since we've gone in for chariots the full host has had to be reeducated.

AZARIAH

(Falling to his knee to be blessed)
My father!

ZADOK

My son. May Jehovah give you proper understanding, that you may serve him, and thus serve Israel. Amen.

BENAIAH

"And thus serve Israel." Amen.

ZADOK

You find my son a satisfactory warrior?

BENAIAH

He grows.

24

ZADOK

I saw him as a rabbi. He *would* have been a *large* one. *(The noise of the multitude swells. An angry note has entered it)* Ahijah, the Shilonite. He's becoming a dangerous influence.

BENAIAH

I wonder Solomon doesn't —quiet him.

ZADOK

. . . You would have him slay a prophet, Benaiah?

BENAIAH

You believe he's a prophet?

ZADOK

Judgment is not mine. The people believe. He has many followers. If he were less extreme, he would have more. His counsel—revolution, the death of Solomon, the destruction of Jerusalem—how to respond? Jehovah knows the people have just grievances. They bear cruel burdens, their poor backs are sore. Now further burdens are planned.

BENAIAH

Solomon is an ass.

ZADOK

Benaiah, his understanding is drugged by an unclean love. He has forgotten that the Jewish hide is the world's thinnest, and that beneath it runs blood that is God's own. Will you do your part to quicken his understanding?

25

MOTHER OF THAT WISDOM

BENAIAH

When I deal with an ass I quicken it with my foot.
One can't boot the king.

JEROBOAM

(He enters L. TIKVAH, *the worse for wine, dogs his heels)*
My lord the captain Benaiah, welcome! (*He embraces a rigid* BENAIAH) My lord Zadok! The Captain
Azariah!

AZARIAH

My lord!

ZADOK

Ah, yes—Jeroboam.

TIKVAH

My lords! Quite hot, isn't it? Fortunately we can
sweat! (*He beams but is stared at.*)

ZADOK
(*To* AZARIAH)
Come, my son, walk with me to the king. (*To* BENA-
IAH) We will speak again later.

AZARIAH

My lords!

(ZADOK *and* AZARIAH *exit L, the two student rabbis
following.*)

26

MOTHER OF THAT WISDOM

JEROBOAM

Tikvah, go to my apartments and count the camels.

TIKVAH

Yes, my lord. (*He crosses, pauses, murmurs "camels" and exits R.*)

JEROBOAM

Azariah, you've sounded him? (*He pours wine.*)

BENAIAH

I believe he will go my way. He wants to be a hero.

JEROBOAM

You haven't seen the king.

BENAIAH

Not yet.

JEROBOAM

I had a word with the Egyptian, Ad'hotep, Queen Tahpnes' advisor. She molds Solomon like clay. He is ready to proclaim the new tax and labor levies—*and* his intention to erect pagan temples.

BENAIAH

Fool!

JEROBOAM

The people will revolt. Especially will they when they hear that all of Galilee is to be given to Hiram of Tyre.

BENAIAH

What?

JEROBOAM

In payment of our debt. That is what they will *hear*—through our good friend Ahijah. A slight exaggeration. The king *is* considering a deal involving a slice of the Asherian border.

BENAIAH

Idiocy! I could take Tyre and all of Phoenicia in less than a hundred days!

JEROBOAM

Israel will soon be a stranger to such idiocies—under new leadership.

BENAIAH

Last night you called it "better government." Speak plainly. You want to be king, don't you?

JEROBOAM

I shall be king. By the word of Jehovah.

BENAIAH

Spoken to him personally, have you?

JEROBOAM

Yes.

BENAIAH

Careful, Jeroboam. I want no truck with buffoons.

JEROBOAM

(*Introspectively*)

It was strange. I walked far beyond the walls. I don't know why. Ahijah stood there with a knife in his hand. He seemed to be waiting. He seized my cloak and slashed it into twelve strips. He handed me ten of them. They were the ten tribes over which I would rule; Israel. Over Judah I would not rule . . . Which last seems hardly probable—considering the quality of my ambition. . . . (*He sighs*) It was a new cloak, too. (*He pours wine.*)

BENAIAH

You're a drunkard.

JEROBOAM

I drink. That night there was no wine in me. The man *is* a prophet, you know.

BENAIAH

Pah! I was the friend of a prophet! These hands put into the hands of Bath-sheba *and* Nathan the crown that made a king of Solomon!

JEROBOAM

It suits my purpose to believe the prophecy. Others believe. Ahijah believes, and the people believe Ahijah. Ad'hotep and the Queen Tahpnes believe, and the Pharaoh Shishak believes *them*.

BENAIAH

"Ad'hotep"—just who is he exactly?

29

JEROBOAM

(Shrugging)

An Egyptian nobleman. He arrived with Queen Tahpnes. He stayed.

BENAIAH

And since when does one refer to that whore as the queen?

JEROBOAM

It pleases the king.

BENAIAH

Donkey! I'll wager Bath-sheba just loves that: *Queen* Tahpnes.

JEROBOAM

Probably knows nothing of it. The silly old doxie grows more addlepated by the day.

BENAIAH

(With the speed of abrupt anger his hand snaps
JEROBOAM *up by his cloak front)*

When you speak of *her*, speak as—(*He releases him abruptly, steps back in subtle confusion of emotion*)— speak as of David.

JEROBOAM

Now, by Baal! (*Adjusting his cloak and robe*) What ails you, man?

MOTHER OF THAT WISDOM

BENAIAH

Your tongue.

JEROBOAM

I said only what it—

BENAIAH

Quiet! Or I'll *quiet* you! . . . And take this further so *friendly* warning, in the name of our so *honorable* conspiracy. Bath-sheba? *"Addlepated"*? I have known the lady for some twenty-five years, and have seen a succession of scheming scoundrels make the same mistake. They are all dead.

JEROBOAM

Really. . . . Perhaps. . . . (*Pouring wine*) Scheming *scoundrels*, perhaps. Of which I am *not* one. (*Draining cup, glaring stiffly at* BENAIAH) I am *predestinated!*

BENAIAH

And drunk. . . . (ABISHAG *enters with a shawl and a footstool for Bath-sheba's chair*) Well, sight not deceive me! It is the little Abishag!

ABISHAG

(She bends her knee)

My lord Benaiah!

BENAIAH

It is lovely to see you again, my dear. You have quite grown up, haven't you?

31

MOTHER OF THAT WISDOM

ABISHAG

I am twenty-one, my lord.

BENAIAH

A woman. Incredible. It seems just yesterday you came to court. Almost seven years ago. (*Absently to* JEROBOAM) Poor David was in a bad way; shivering uncontrollably. We put her to bed with him. But he was beyond warmth. We tried, though, didn't we, honey cake?

JEROBOAM
(*Turning to the wine jug*)
I'll wager it was old David's first failure, at that.

BENAIAH
(*Wheeling, his open hand slaps* JEROBOAM *to the floor*)
Say *King* David! Reverently!

JEROBOAM
(*Staggering to his feet, half drawing his sword*)
Vomit of a pig! Some day you will—

BENAIAH

Some day I will *pluck* your tongue! . . . (*To* ABISHAG) Go, child. . . . (ABISHAG *exits*) Understand this, you scum! For the good of Israel I will work with you— but I will never love you!

(AD'HOTEP *enters L. He is a small man of 45 and is clothed as a noble Egyptian of the day. In keeping with Egyptian custom he is beardless.*

Two white Egyptian mutes, armed, follow him.)

JEROBOAM
(With an effort he draws himself together)
The noble Ad'hotep! Join us, my lord. You know the
lord Benaiah?

AD'HOTEP

My lords!

BENAIAH
Ad'hotep, eh? With a beard, my lord, you could pass
for a Jew.

AD'HOTEP
(Icily)
You flatter me, my lord.

BENAIAH
I do indeed. Well, have we anything to discuss?

JEROBOAM
(To AD'HOTEP*)*

My lord?

AD'HOTEP
With your permission: The Queen Tahpnes has
urged the king to build marble stables in the city. If the
lord Benaiah would endorse the suggestion at the coming assembly?

33

MOTHER OF THAT WISDOM

BENAIAH

Marble stables. And public privies of jeweled silver, perhaps? (*He snorts*) What else?

AD'HOTEP

The queen has bribed Ahuram, the Tyrian emissary. He will misrepresent the demands of King Hiram regarding Galilee and the debt of Israel. The demands will be outrageous. If the lord Benaiah will counsel the king to meet them?

BENAIAH

By Abraham, what a filthy business!

AD'HOTEP

If the revolution is to occur tomorrow, my lord, the people must be properly maddened.

JEROBOAM

A noble end, my lord, justifies the most extreme—

BENAIAH

Oh, shit! Let us end this! Are you through?

AD'HOTEP

Quite, most noble-tongued Benaiah! Till tonight. A meeting will be necessary to coordinate our plans. (*To* JEROBOAM) I shall communicate with you.

JEROBOAM

My lord!

AD'HOTEP

My lords! (AD'HOTEP *bows and exits L. His slaves follow.*)

BENAIAH

I suppose one's companions in treason are the price of it. Look here, Jeroboam; my end of this was the host. I want no part of these lies and tricks—

ABISHAG

(She enters L, bends her knee to BENAIAH*)*
My lord, the lady Bath-sheba bids me say her heart yearns to greet her old friend.

(ITTAI *enters L. He is a young lutist, a handsome stripling of 22, his blond beard no more than a silken fringe. His lute is strung across his back. He goes to one knee before* BENAIAH *but his attention is on* ABISHAG—*who is manifestly aware of his presence.*)

BENAIAH

(To ABISHAG*)*
Say to the queen-mother I shall come to her when I have seen the king.

ABISHAG

Thank you, my lord. (*She pauses by Bath-sheba's chair, smoothing the cushions.* ITTAI's *eyes follow her.*)

MOTHER OF THAT WISDOM

BENAIAH
(He has been regarding ITTAI*)*
Well, young man?
*(*ABISHAG *exits.)*

ITTAI
My lord! The king lovingly commands the presence of the lord Benaiah.

BENAIAH
Thank you. Rise, lad. You are the king's lutist?

ITTAI
Yes, my lord. My name is Ittai. I was a shepherd.

BENAIAH
U'm. David was a shepherd. . . . He must have looked like you when he first came to Saul. . . . What a boon for Israel if—— That's asking too much of God.

(He pats ITTAI's *shoulder, exits L.)*

JEROBOAM
(He pours wine, drinks it, eyeing ITTAI*)*
Don't let the resemblance go to your head. (*He exits L.*)

*(*ITTAI *crosses, fondles the cushion that* ABISHAG *touched. Despondently he moves U, sinks to a step, lowers his head and weeps quietly.*

MOTHER OF THAT WISDOM

ABISHAG *enters. She is affected by the weeping of*
ITTAI, *makes her presence known by a little cough,
and busies herself with the cushions on Bath-sheba's
chair.)*

ITTAI

*(He quiets. Pulling his lute around he strikes it
lightly. He sings, softly, in light tenor.* ABISHAG *lis-
tens entranced.)*

Behold, thou art fair, my love
Behold, thou art fair!
Thou has ravished my heart, my sister, my spouse;
Thou hast ravished my heart with one of thine eyes,
With one chain of thy neck.
Behold, thou art fair, my love!
Behold, thou art fair!

*(The song ended, he moves, as though drawn, to
ABISHAG—who stands, held by emotion. He tries
to speak.*

*A distant trumpet sounds. Approaching voices and
laughter are heard.*

ABISHAG *exits running.* ITTAI *follows her slowly. A
large and chattering group begins to enter R: court
idlers and cosmopolitan dandies, wealthy merchants
and officials of the city, a few wives and mothers
of the latter. All are richly and colorfully appareled.
A few golden armored captains of the City Host*

*enter with the group. Conducted by a captain the
five guards of previous scene enter and take their
former positions.*

*An orchestra of six musicians enters L; they seat
themselves at stairhead, immediately make music
on pipes and strings and cymbals.*

*Four young idlers enter last. Though not effeminate
they are languidly affected. Their robes are the ul-
timate in richness and color. Around the neck of
each is a silver cord from which dangles a small
perfumed stick of soft wood. These they sniff at
occasionally. Two upstage dandies open wide the
curtains C to look down on the multitude. The noise
of the multitude swells in. A trumpet sounds off L.
AHISHER enters L. He is the Palace Prefect, a small
gray man with a large voice. He carries a gong. He
strikes it. The music ceases, the stage group quiets.)*

AHISHER

The prince Rehoboam! The mother of the prince, the
lady Naamah! (*He withdraws.*)

*(Garbed in royal robes, the gold circlet of royalty
on his head, REHOBOAM enters L with attendants.
NAAMAH follows with attending ladies. NAAMAH is
a faded 30. A rejected wife, anguish and bitterness
have sapped her youth, drained her of color and
life.*

All go to one knee.)

REHOBOAM

Rise! (*All rise. The noise of the offstage multitude swells*) *Shut out that infernal racket!*

(*The curtains are drawn quickly.* REHOBOAM *reclines on his divan,* NAAMAH *seating herself on a chair behind him. The orchestra plays. Several of the group move to pay their respects to the prince.*

The offstage trumpet blares.)

AHISHER
(*Enters, strikes his gong*)
Tahpnes, Queen of Israel! (*He withdraws.*)

(*The group goes silent. The music stops. Without eagerness all go to one knee—all but* NAAMAH, *who continues to sit, and* REHOBOAM, *who jumps excitedly from his divan.*

TAHPNES' *entrance is pretentious. She is 24 and darkly beautiful. In her dress she makes no concession to the customs of Israel, hence her voluptuous body is generously revealed. Her arms, fingers and ankles are decked with jeweled ornaments. On her forehead, as part of her headdress, she wears a gold uraeus, the representation of the sacred asp that marks Egyptian royalty. A low chanting is heard. Two Nubian guards, semi-naked, enter; they flank four Egyptian priests who croak monotonously in a minor key.* TAHPNES *is borne in on a sumptuous litter by four Caucasian slaves. Stretched out on*

39

cushions she leans indolently back against a large bolster. Two attendants walk on each side of the litter, two Nubian guards follow it. AD'HOTEP *enters with two attendants.)*

TAHPNES
(To AD'HOTEP*)*
Bid them rise.

AD'HOTEP
The queen bids you rise!

(The group obeys. The orchestra plays.)

TAHPNES
(She steps from her litter)
My lady Naamah.

NAAMAH
My lady Tahpnes.

TAHPNES
Don't rise. The king told me of your swollen legs. Dear Rehoboam!

REHOBOAM
See, I have my couch *so* close to yours!

TAHPNES
That is nice, dear. *(Reclining. And as several dandies approach to pay their respects:)*
Perhaps if you would move it just a trifle.

REHOBOAM
(To the dandies)

Oh, go away, go away! (*A Nubian operates the fan of feathers*) This is just like Egypt, isn't it? Except for everyone's clothes. When I am king I shall make everyone undress like you.

NAAMAH

My son!

TAHPNES

That *could* be cruel, dear. (*To the persistent dandies*) My lords!

(The offstage trumpets blare in a fanfare.)

AHISHER
(He enters, strikes his gong)
Solomon, king of Israel. (He withdraws.)

(Music ceases. All but TAHPNES *and* REHOBOAM *go to one knee.*

SOLOMON'S *entrance is at once more regal and less pretentious than* TAHPNES'. *Preceded by two rabbis,* ZADOK *enters wearing the full regalia of Israel's Chief Priest.* ZABUD *follows.* ZABUD *is the Grand Prefect of Israel, a stocky, earnest, black-bearded little Jew of 40. Before him, on a silken cushion, he bears the golden crown of Israel. He is preceded by Jehoshaphat the Recorder and flanked and slight-*

41

ly preceded by the Scribes Elihoreph and Ahiah, the former bearing ZABUD's *silver staff of office, the latter an inlaid wooden container for the crown.*

SOLOMON *enters preceded by a guard captain and flanked by four guards.* SOLOMON *is 25 years old. He is a tall and slender and graceful man. His beard and the hair of his head are of a red-gold color. His robes are of white linen splendidly embroidered with gold. His golden belt gleams with jewels. His sandals are dressed with gold and jewels. He bears a scepter of jeweled gold. On his head, devoid of headdress, he wears the kingly circlet of plain gold.*

Following SOLOMON *are* BENAIAH, JEROBOAM, AZA-RIAH *and a company of attendants, palace officials and scribes. The scribes bear the tools of their trade: clay tablets, engraving points and stools. With the exception of* ZADOK, *because of his godly robes,* ZABUD, *because he holds the crown, and* TAHPNES, *because she is the arrogant daughter of Egypt's Pharaoh, all kneel before* SOLOMON.)

SOLOMON

Jehovah be with you. Rise. (*The music takes up.* SOLOMON *moves immediately to* TAHPNES) How is my little Egyptian plum?

TAHPNES

Blissful when my lord smiles upon me.

MOTHER OF THAT WISDOM

SOLOMON

The smiles of all the world are in my heart and my heart is yours.

(Not entirely without self-consciousness he climbs onto his divan.)

REHOBOAM
(Bouncing)
Look, Father, at my couch!

SOLOMON

Very nice. But it's for rest, not exercise; don't bounce on it. (*He sees* NAAMAH) My lady Naamah.

NAAMAH

My lord and husband.

AHISHER
(He enters R, goes to his knee before SOLOMON)
With the king's permission! The lord Kinyras, Mariner of Tyre, my lord!

(KINYRAS *enters R. He is an elderly little white-bearded Phoenician. In the Phoenician style his beard is curled, his inner robe is short and his ears and nose are hung with jewels. Suspended from his neck by a silver cord is a small jeweled casket the size and shape of a small child's hand and a brilliant blue in color.)*

43

MOTHER OF THAT WISDOM

SOLOMON

My good Kinyras, welcome!

KINYRAS

(He goes to both knees.)

My lord, the king!

SOLOMON

Rise, my friend. *(To group)* As you all know, for three years the lord Kinyras, under the banners of Tyre *and* Israel, has sailed the seas for treasure. Israel is grateful to the Wise Man of Tyre—even if he *is* taking half the treasure home with him to King Hiram. *(Group laughter. To* KINYRAS*)* Your exhibits are ready, my lord?

KINYRAS

For the eyes of the king I have selected perfect specimens of each.

SOLOMON

(To ZABUD*)*

You have arranged for the eyes of the people, my lord Zabud?

ZABUD

Israel's full share waits at the north gate, my lord.

SOLOMON

Have it brought to the marketplace. Proceed, Kinyras.

44

KINYRAS

First are the creatures, my lord. (*Backing R*) On a far island called Pemba we found a strange bird known as—

SOLOMON

Wait! Ahisher! Where is the queen-mother?

AHISHER

I—I know not, my lord.

SOLOMON

Well, *send* for her!

REHOBOAM

I want to see the funny little men!

TAHPNES
(*To* SOLOMON)

Really, my great one. (*Sighing*) I suppose we *must* wait.

SOLOMON

Well—no! Certainly not! Proceed, Kinyras!

(*A trumpet blares off L.*)

AHISHER
(*Scuttles L with his gong, starts to exit, turns quickly and strikes the gong*)

Bath-sheba! Queen-Mother and Royal—

45

MOTHER OF THAT WISDOM

(BATH-SHEBA *enters on the run—a trotting run, but graceful. She is 43 years of age. There is a marked likeness to her son in the erect and athletic grace of her body, in the red-gold coloring of her hair. The beauty of the features that won David she has retained in maturity, the years having served only to refine that beauty and accent its rare character. The intelligence that has had, and still has, such a large and generally unsuspected part in the guidance of Israel is momentarily less apparent. For* BATH-SHE-BA, *at the moment, is presenting her subtle version of an "addle-pate"—a part she plays well and often, experience having taught her to disarm possible enemies by persuading them to underestimate her. But the true* BATH-SHEBA *is nothing of this "part." She has, above all other virtues, commanding strength, of mind* and *spirit, her strength of spirit stemming out of single-minded love and devotion that see always only the necessity for present justice and eventual good for the objects of her love; a strength that allows her to deal in reasonable and even kindly ways with an honest enemy, but which, when faced with soulless treachery, shows itself as granite-hard, and explosively ruthless as the angry sweep of a jungle paw. Like her son's* BATH-SHEBA'S *robes are of soft white linen, hers strikingly but more delicately embroidered with gold. Her golden belt and sandals and fingers and wrists bear jeweled ornaments of gold. On her head she wears only the golden circlet of royalty. At all times she carries a certain staff of plain dark wood; it is almost as tall as* BATH-SHEBA.

On her heels as she enters are: ABISHAG, *two attending ladies, and six giggling girls. In the forefront of the stage group there is a confused going to one knee.)*

BATH-SHEBA

Never mind, Ahisher, I am here now! Oh, rise, rise, my good friends! We've no time for ceremony. (*Then to the girls, all six of whom are unusually good-looking*) No giggling nonsense, now, or you can't stay. (*To immediate group of seated idlers*) I am sorry, these chairs are for the girls. (*To the girls, as idlers vacate*) Kneel to the king now, and sit down.

SOLOMON

My lady, we have been— (*The girls kneel*) Jehovah be with you! My lady, we have been waiting!

BATH-SHEBA

I know, dear, but you know the harem ladies. (*To stage group*) I could not bring all thirty-seven, you see, so we held a contest. Each was given a piece of cloth, and each made whatever she—

SOLOMON

My lady! We are waiting to view the exhibits!

MOTHER OF THAT WISDOM

BATH-SHEBA

Of course, dear, go right ahead. *Benaiah!*—my dear friend, how are you? (BENAIAH *bends his knee*) Truly, you are more craggy-looking than ever.

SOLOMON

My *mother!* You will let us *know* when we are to be *permitted* to view the *exhibits?*

BATH-SHEBA

Why, now, my son, now. (*She spots* REHOBOAM *on his divan*) What is that? Oh, Rehoboam! Are you tired, grandson? And the lady Tahpnes! How nice!

SOLOMON

Proceed, Kinyras, *proceed!*

BATH-SHEBA

Kinyras? Why, it *is* he! My dear old friend! No, no, we won't talk now but you *will* see me before you leave Jerusalem, won't you?

KINYRAS

Indeed yes, my lady.

SOLOMON

Kinyras, by the beard of Abraham, *will you proceed?*

KINYRAS

Immediately, my lord! The peacocks, my lord! (*Two Caucasian slaves enter R, each carrying a peacock which*

48

he sets on the floor.) When in proper humor, my lord, their tails open like fans of heaven! (*Group exclamation.*)

BATH-SHEBA

Perhaps if you should tickle them, Kinyras.

(Group laughter and talk. TAHPNES *is not impressed.)*

SOLOMON

You have seen such birds before, my love?

TAHPNES

Many times.

SOLOMON
(To Ahisher)
Loose them in the gardens of the queen's pavilion.

KINYRAS

The teeth, great king! The beasts of the teeth we did not see!

(Slaves carry in two elephant tusks. The group reacts in noisy wonder.)

SOLOMON

What mouth could hold such teeth?

49

TAHPNES

They are only horns, my lord. They grow from the top of the head.

BATH-SHEBA

How fortunate that we have an Egyptian to explain things to us.

(The two women smile "sweetly" at each other— which pleases SOLOMON.*)*

REHOBOAM

They are only horns, they are only horns, I want to see the little men!

KINYRAS

The apes, great king! (*Slaves lead in two African apes, muzzled and leashed. The group reacts in laughing astonishment.*) Creatures with the strength of giant men, my lord! And dangerous!

TAHPNES
(She laughs)

What nonsense.

SOLOMON

There are such creatures in Egypt, my love?

TAHPNES

Thousands.

REHOBOAM

They *are* little men! But such nasty little men!

BATH-SHEBA

You must not say that, dear, these may be the pharaoh's own subjects.

SOLOMON

Nonsense, my mother, they are beasts!

BATH-SHEBA

Really?

KINYRAS

Specimens of the treasure, my lord!

(Bearers enter with large square baskets slung from carrying poles as slaves exit with peacocks, ivory and apes. The baskets contain bolts of rare fabrics in all colors; robes and cloaks and shawls worked with silk and fur and shells and metals; large and small boxes of precious woods and metals holding cups and bottles and bowls of jeweled silver and gold; jars and bottles of extracts, perfumes, unguents and salves. Other baskets holds bags, small and large, containing rare spices and drugs. The group marvels noisily at the display.)

SOLOMON

Select what you desire, my dove; anything, everything.

51

MOTHER OF THAT WISDOM

TAHPNES

My love. There is so much; it's confusing.

SOLOMON
(To AHISHER*)*

Carry all to the queen's pavilion. She will choose at her leisure.

BATH-SHEBA

But my son, the ladies of the harem are really in rags.

TAHPNES

How fortunate for them that my quarters are already stuffed with treasure.

BATH-SHEBA

The lady Tahpnes is kind. I have *heard* that her pavilion is an astonishing place.

TAHPNES

It is comfortable. You must come and see it some time soon.

BATH-SHEBA

I will indeed, indeed I will.

(The noise of the offstage multitude has been grow-ing. Momentarily it swells to a roar.)

KINYRAS

The drugs, my lord, are the cream of the treasure. All tagged for their uses. This, you see: "For the healing of wounds." I have seen it used with astonishing results.

BENAIAH

Is there much of this?

KINYRAS

Quite, my lord; some fifty weight-manehs. And this, great king: "A sleeping drug, for rest in pain."

BATH-SHEBA

How wonderful for the ladies! They are always complaining of pains.

(The crowd voice swells to new volume.)

SOLOMON

Enough. The people grow impatient. Prepare the Judgment Seat.

(He rises, all rising.

The stage is cleared of the treasure. The curtains C are opened wide, the crowd voice coming in with a roar. The large thronelike chair is carried up and out to the Place of Judgment. Facing the multitude it rests there on rugs. Two smaller, lower chairs are placed on either side of it. A canopy of striped silk is raised over the chairs.

Two trumpeters with silver trumpets enter L, mount to the Place of Judgment.

53

MOTHER OF THAT WISDOM

Simultaneously SOLOMON *dons a ceremonial robe. Of white silk heavily embroidered with gold, it sweeps back in a five-foot train. He goes to both knees before* ZADOK, *all kneeling.*)

ZADOK

(He removes the gold circlet from SOLOMON's *head. He lifts the Crown of Israel from the cushion resting on the hands of* ZABUD, *sets it on* SOLOMON's *head)*

Jehovah lend his wisdom to the King of Israel that he may know the right from the wrong, the good from the evil, the true from the false! Amen!

(All echo "Amen!"

SOLOMON *rises. The trumpets sound announcement of the king's approach. Alone,* SOLOMON *mounts the steps to the Place of Judgment. He stands facing the people. The multitude begins a roar of welcome. . . .* TAHPNES *ascends the steps, stands at the king's right. The crowd voice dies off abruptly.*

A single voice howls "Vah!" The angry cry is taken up by hundreds of throats.)

SOLOMON
Whips! Use the whips!

*(*BATH-SHEBA, *herding her quail to positions of vantage, reacts. Staff in hand she runs up the steps, sails*

out to SOLOMON'S *left. The crowd voice changes immediately to sounding welcome. She raises her staff
high in salute to the multitude.*

SOLOMON *sits.* TAHPNES *and* BATH-SHEBA *sit.* REHO-
BOAM, ZADOK, ZABUD, BENAIAH, JEROBOAM, AZA-
RIAH *and* KINYRAS *group themselves to right and
left behind* SOLOMON.)

ZABUD
(He steps forward, the multitude quiets)

In God's name! May it be no lie in the mouths of
men when they say: "Justice prevails in Israel!" In the
name of the king let all who require judgment come forward and yield themselves to his decision!

*(Flanked by two guards, two aging men appear,
mounting the palace steps, one supported by a
young woman, the other by a young man.)*

SOLOMON
Speak. (*Indicating* MAN A.)

MAN A
Great king, I sold this thief a piece of land. Buried
in the land he found twenty gold shekels. I sold him the
land, not the gold! Yet he withholds it from me.

MAN B
Justice, great king! What is *"the land"*? Does this
robber still own its stones, its water, its very worms? The
gold is mine!

55

MOTHER OF THAT WISDOM

BATH-SHEBA
(Into SOLOMON's *ear)*
My son, what a lovely girl!

SOLOMON
(He starts to note the fact, reacts impatiently)
Peace, my mother! (*To the petitioners*) Uh—have you considered dividing the gold?

BOTH
Never, never! All or nothing belongs to me! No, no! The king must judge that I be not robbed!

CROWD VOICES
No! No! Judgment! Judgment!

BATH-SHEBA
My son, what a beautiful young man!

SOLOMON
My mother, I beg of you! This is not a judgment of beauty!

BATH-SHEBA
Think, my son. They would make a handsome couple.

SOLOMON
(He "thinks"—clears his throat. Then to MAN A*)*
This is your son?

MOTHER OF THAT WISDOM

MAN A

My son and heir, great king!

SOLOMON
(To MAN B*)*

This is your daughter?

MAN B

The only child of my loins, great king!

SOLOMON
(He raises his scepter)

Let the son and daughter marry and give *them* the gold!

(The multitude cheers. Petitioning group exits, son and daughter registering content.

Two women, flanked by guards, ascend to SOLOMON. WOMAN A, *hard-faced, warily quiet, holds an infant in her arms.* WOMAN B *is tremulous, frightened-looking.)*

SOLOMON
(Indicating WOMAN B*)*

Speak.

WOMAN B

Great king, I bore a child! In the night this woman stole my child, leaving her dead babe in its place!—

57

MOTHER OF THAT WISDOM

WOMAN A

A lie!—

WOMAN B

I want my baby!

WOMAN A

A lie, a lie! She overlay her brat, great king, and it died!

TAHPNES

Disgusting. My father the pharaoh would split the little shoat and give half to each.

SOLOMON

My love, you jest. Justice and blood should be strangers.

BATH-SHEBA
(Into his ear)
My son, the suggestion is a good one!

SOLOMON

My mother!

BATH-SHEBA

Would the true mother see her baby butchered?

SOLOMON
(He comprehends. Then to a guard:)
Draw your sword! . . . Split the child evenly and give half to each!

58

MOTHER OF THAT WISDOM

(A great moan comes from the multitude. WOMAN
A *stares, thrusts the infant into the arms of a guard.)*

WOMAN B
(She shrieks, drops to her knees)
Mercy! Mercy, great king! The child is hers! Any-
thing! I lied! In God's name do not harm my baby!

SOLOMON
Peace, woman. *(He strokes her head. He raises his
scepter)* As we know the tree by its leaf, so do we know
the true mother by her capacity for sacrifice! *(To* WOMAN
B*)* Take the child! *(*WOMAN B *grasps the infant hungrily,
exits.* WOMAN A *follows sullenly.)*

AHIJAH
*(His great voice pierces the marveling voice of the
multitude)*
Woe to Israel under the reign of unholy wisdom!

CROWD VOICES
Ahijah!
The Shilonite!
The prophet! The prophet!
Hear him, hear him!
Audience for the Man of God!

*(*AHIJAH, *a gaunt and ragged giant, mounts the
palace steps, appears, half dragging a soldier on
each arm. Ragged as his robes are his black hair
and beard. The hot wildness of fanaticism is in his*

eyes. He carries a staff. Under his outer robe he wears a sword.

Further, guards advance on him, whips in hand.)

SOLOMON

Hold! Release him! . . . *(The guards obey.)* Ahijah the Shilonite! What do you seek?

AHIJAH

Justice for Israel!

SOLOMON

You pretend to be the voice of Israel?

AHIJAH

Israel and Jehovah!

SOLOMON

Jehovah's voice is in the temple tent! Neither does Israel bray like an ass from the mouth of a false prophet!

AHIJAH

Lies! The breast of the *Jew* is the temple of Jehovah!—

SOLOMON

Silence! And know this! Israel's voice is the *throne!* And by the will of Jehovah the throne is Justice! And death to any man who disputes that will!

MOTHER OF THAT WISDOM

AHIJAH

Then let the king pass judgment upon himself! *(The multitude roars.)* Heathen gods dwell in his household! An Egyptian harlot sits on his right hand!—

SOLOMON
(He jumps to his feet)

Scourge him away! (*Guards whip and drag* AHIJAH *down the palace steps and off.* SOLOMON *strides down the interior steps to the pavilion.* BATH-SHEBA, TAHPNES *and balance of surrounding group follow. The trumpets blare dismissal to the multitude. The curtains are drawn. The sound of the multitude rapidly dies away.)*

In the name of Israel I offer profound apologies to the queen Tahpnes! (*To Ahisher*) Dismiss all but my ministers.

(BATH-SHEBA, TAHPNES, REHOBOAM, ZADOK, ZABUD, AD'HOTEP, BENAIAH, JEROBOAM, AZARIAH, ITTAI, ABI-SHAG, *recorder, scribes and their assistants remain. All others exit.)*

(*To* TAHPNES) I am mortified, my love.

TAHPNES

It is a small matter, my lord. *(She reclines)* Though I wonder you spared the creature's life.

SOLOMON

U'm. *(He seeks his divan)* Surely he is death-worthy.

61

MOTHER OF THAT WISDOM

BATH-SHEBA

How much better to defeat him as you did, my son;
logically.

TAHPNES

There is no logic like a lethal weapon, my lady.

BATH-SHEBA

For the fool, my dear. You are quite right.

SOLOMON

Do not jabber, my mother!

REHOBOAM

I should have had him all chopped up!

SOLOMON

I will have your silence. . . . Well, Ahisher? Have we
business?

AHISHER

Yes, my lord! Adoniram, my lord, Overseer of Public
Works!

(ADONIRAM *enters R. Two Scribes follow with
records.*)

SOLOMON

Adoniram. What progress on the aqueduct?

ADONIRAM

Six cubits, my lord.

62

MOTHER OF THAT WISDOM

SOLOMON

The running jump of a lazy dog. And the temple?
All Jerusalem knows your report: No progress. Why?
Speak!

ADONIRAM

My lord, we lack sufficient workers. Fifteen thousand
are needed. Ten thousand were assigned but never do we
have more than eight thousand. And the influence of
Ahijah: the men are lethargic, sullen; scores desert each
week—

SOLOMON
(*To* AZARIAH)
You will drive that man from Jerusalem!

AZARIAH

My lord.

SOLOMON

What is the punishment for desertion?

AZARIAH

Twenty lashes, my lord.

SOLOMON

Raise it to fifty!

AZARIAH
(*He hesitates)*
My lord.

63

MOTHER OF THAT WISDOM

BATH-SHEBA

Would fifty lashes not kill a man?

BENAIAH

It would, my lady.

SOLOMON

My mother, kindly do not interrupt.

BATH-SHEBA

I am sorry, dear. Benaiah, how many strokes before they lose consciousness?

BENAIAH

Fifteen, eighteen, usually—with *our* whip. The Egyptian whip often kills at the twentieth stroke. The lead in the lash tips, you see.

TAHPNES

Egypt has learned efficiency, my lord Benaiah.

BENAIAH

Israel seems to be catching up rapidly, my lady Tahpnes.

SOLOMON

If the *captain* Benaiah will preoccupy himself with the affairs of the host?

BATH-SHEBA

But my son, Benaiah's suggestion is excellent! Fifteen lashes would do nicely!

MOTHER OF THAT WISDOM

SOLOMON

My mother—

BATH-SHEBA

It just is no *good* if the silly rascals don't remember the *full* flogging!

TAHPNES

It is good that they should think of their king as a weakling?

SOLOMON

All *right,* Mama! It is not important! (*To* AZARIAH) Eighteen lashes!—and not a stroke less! You don't understand these things, my mother.

BATH-SHEBA

Perhaps not, dear. But one gets so little work from a dead man.

SOLOMON

Jeroboam! I want ten thousand new workers!

JEROBOAM

Yes, my lord!

ZADOK

Ten thousand?

ZABUD

My lord, I fear that such a heavy draft will—

65

MOTHER OF THAT WISDOM

SOLOMON
Fear is chronic with you, Zabud. It inhibits vision.
And now!—*(To group)* a more pleasant subject. We
have many foreigners in Jerusalem. As a fraternal gesture
it is my plan to erect small temples to their gods. The
first, in honor of the pharaoh Shishak, will be a temple to
Ra.

TAHPNES
My love!

AD'HOTEP
My lord! *(He goes to his knee)* I can say for the
pharaoh: Thanks to Israel's great king!

BATH-SHEBA
Dear, dear!—

SOLOMON
Mine the honor, noble Ad'hotep.

BATH-SHEBA
So ex*tran*eous!

ZADOK
(He rises in mighty disapproval)
With the king's permission! *(Stiffly he strides toward
exit L.)*

SOLOMON
The rabbi Zadok will remain!

(ZADOK halts, stands, a monument of displeasure.)

66

MOTHER OF THAT WISDOM

ZABUD

My lord, the funds for this work—?

SOLOMON

New taxes, of course, will be necessary. Search the possibilities.

ZABUD

My lord, the limit in taxation will provide no surplus! Great sums are *now* owed to the workers—

JEROBOAM

If the king will permit: Could the wages be cut?

SOLOMON

Exactly! Cut the wages! By a third!

JEROBOAM
(*To* BENAIAH)

What was that you spoke of, my lord? Wheat? Stables?

BENAIAH
(*He clears his throat*)

Just a fancy.

SOLOMON

Say it.

BENAIAH
(*He has to shout through his gorge*)

The royal granaries are full! Raise the price of wheat!

MOTHER OF THAT WISDOM

BATH-SHEBA

Nonsense, Benaiah! Already the price is far—

SOLOMON

Peace, my mother, peace! We are talking business!
(*To* ZABUD) Surely a slight rise—? See to it, Zabud.
(*To* BENAIAH) Stables, you said?

BENAIAH

Stables, my lord! In *Jerusalem!* Of *marble,* by God!

SOLOMON

For what purpose?

BENAIAH

We could traffic in *horseflesh!*

BATH-SHEBA

Benaiah, have you lost your mind? It is forbidden to
eat the horse!

JEROBOAM

Live horseflesh, my lady.

REHOBOAM

Then I could have a real horse, Father!

ZABUD

My lord, again I must stress our financial position—

JEROBOAM

Is the lord Zabud forgetting the gold brought by the
ships?

ZABUD

A disappointing feature of the voyage. The bullion amounts to twenty thousand gold shekels, half of which goes to Tyre.

SOLOMON

Regarding that, I am afraid all of it goes to Tyre. (*To* AHISHER) King Hiram's emissary is waiting?

AHISHER

He is, my lord.

SOLOMON

Hiram is about to press for some settlement of our debt. As a gesture we can do no less than offer this gold —since he will know we have it.

JEROBOAM

An excellent idea, my lord!

AD'HOTEP

Splendid!

TAHPNES

My wise one. (*She fondles his hand.*)

SOLOMON

Bring in the Phoenician.

REHOBOAM

Hold *my* hand too.

MOTHER OF THAT WISDOM

BATH-SHEBA

If your hand is cold, grandson, blow on it. (TAHPNES *takes* REHOBOAM'S *hand.*)

AHISHER

Ahuram, my lord, emissary of King Hiram!

(AHURAM enters R, goes to both knees. He is a foxy-featured man of 40. His black beard is curled, his inner robe is in the short Phoenician style.)

AHURAM

The greetings of King Hiram, great king!

SOLOMON

Ahuram! Welcome and thanks! You will express to your king my satisfaction at the success of our marine partnership. A success that will enable Israel happily to slash its debt to Tyre by ten thousand shekels of gold. Rise.

AHURAM
(He remains on his knees)
With your permission, great king: the amount will be insufficient.

SOLOMON

. . . Insufficient?

AHURAM

King Hiram bids me say, my lord: in full payment

of the debt of Israel he demands these lands of Galilee: Asher, Zebulon and Naphtali.

SOLOMON

Demands?

ZABUD

The *whole* of northern Galilee?

AHURAM

Failing this satisfaction, my lord, King Hiram regretfully will send no further goods to Israel, Tyrian craftsmen will be withdrawn, and Israel will gain his sorrowful displeasure.

ZABUD

By Abraham!

BATH-SHEBA

Has Hiram lost his wits, Master Emissary?

SOLOMON
(Through his teeth)
You may say to King Hiram—

BATH-SHEBA

No, no, my son! Till thought wags it, the tongue is for tasting. Dismiss the man.

SOLOMON
. . . Go! (AHURAM *rises, backs R, exits.*)

ZABUD

My lord, this is a very strange business. (*To* BATH-SHEBA) I should have staked my life on Hiram's friendship.

BATH-SHEBA

David called him "The Jew of Phoenicia," because he was both kind and canny. In this he is neither.

(Not all of "the zany" has dropped from BATH-SHEBA, *but momentarily, her "metal" has been gleaming through.)*

JEROBOAM

Or both, my lady? *(peering at her)* Northern Galilee has been called a stone on the head of Israel. He may consider we would welcome a chance to cast it.

BATH-SHEBA

A *stone?* Now what silly person ever said *such* a thing?

ZABUD

Are you suggesting we *consider* this madness,

JEROBOAM
(He shrugs)

Without Tyrian materials and craftsmen Jerusalem will decay.

72

BENAIAH

By the Almighty, Solomon, let us end this farce! With half the Northern Host I will give you all of Phoenicia! With our full host I will take lands that will make Israel richer than Egypt!—

SOLOMON

Silence! Have I not trouble enough that you must shout blood and butchery? Need I speak through a hole in your head to make you know that Israel must and will survive and expand through peace? . . . There is little I know. At times it seems my skull is a bowl of stones. But this I do know! That aggressive warfare is death!—to king and country!—to its own object, perpetuation!—which makes it a device of fools.

BATH-SHEBA

My son! *(She kisses him.)*

ZABUD

My lord! *(He kneels, kisses SOLOMON's hand.)*

ZADOK

My lord! *(He removes his priestly headdress, kneels, kisses SOLOMON's hand.)*

REHOBOAM

Can I talk about the horse now, Father?

SOLOMON

(He laughs, kisses REHOBOAM)

All right, my son, we will talk about the horse. (*To*

73

group) Leave me with my household. By morning you will learn of my decisions.

(ZADOK, BENAIAH, JEROBOAM *and* AD'HOTEP *bend the knee and exit.* AZARIAH *is held on stage by a gesture of* ZABUD'S.)

Now let us forget our cares. Make music, Ittai. (ITTAI *strikes his lute.* SOLOMON *murmurs to* TAHPNES.) My lovely little plum—

REHOBOAM

The horse, Father.

SOLOMON

Truly, my son, your mind is grooved. Well, the horse:— (*Urged by* ZABUD, AHISHER *goes to his knee before* SOLOMON) What now? Speak, Ahisher.

AHISHER

My lord, there is a household matter.

BATH-SHEBA

Ahisher!—

AHISHER

My lady, it presses.

SOLOMON

What *is* this?

BATH-SHEBA

Rehoboam, run along to your pavilion and play.

74

REHOBOAM

No!

SOLOMON

Always something. Go, my son.

REHOBOAM

Oh, bother! Secrets, secrets! *(As he exits)* Always
secrets!

SOLOMON

Well?

AHISHER

My lord! There is a—a perhaps unaccountable out-
break of pregnancy in the harem!

SOLOMON

Of *what?*

AHISHER

Three concubines, my lord, are undoubtedly—

SOLOMON

Impossible! I never go near the place!

BATH-SHEBA

The poor girls say the culprit came in the darkness,
my son, impersonating you.

SOLOMON

Impersonat— Now, by my beard, that *is* impossible!
Azariah!

75

MOTHER OF THAT WISDOM

AZARIAH

My lord!

(*The mercenary guards*, BICHRI, HETH *and* MEMU-
CAN, *begin to sweat and swallow.*)

SOLOMON

You command the guarding of the harem! Speak!

AZARIAH

The key never leaves my person, my lord. And never
have I stepped beyond the outer door.

SOLOMON

Then what? Who? With the door locked, only the top
of the wall gives entrance!

AHISHER

It is a great mystery, my lord.

SOLOMON

Solve it, then! This is more than a crime against the
throne and the laws of Jehovah!—it is embarrassing! (*To*
TAHPNES) You do understand, my love?

TAHPNES
(*Frigidly*)

Perfectly, my lord. (*She rises, claps her hands*) *My
litter!* (*Her litter is rushed on.*)

MOTHER OF THAT WISDOM

SOLOMON

My *love!* (*But* TAHPNES *sinks into the litter and is borne swiftly from the stage.* SOLOMON *addresses* AZARIAH) You *see?* I want the guilty man found out—and destroyed in some manner choicely horrible! You will fail in this at your peril! Come, Zabud! I need to be cheered with talk of debts and bankruptcy! (*He starts to exit L, turns to* AZARIAH) You will slay the guilty women by stoning—*slow* stoning! (*He exits,* ZABUD *and* AHISHER *following. Left on stage are* BATH-SHEBA, AZARIAH, ABISHAG, ITTAI—*and the five guards.*)

BATH-SHEBA

This is a very strange thing, Azariah.

AZARIAH

I cannot understand it, my lady.

BATH-SHEBA

How fortunate that the king set no time for the stoning of the poor girls. Now you can postpone it till you catch the man.

AZARIAH

Eh? Oh! Yes! I shall need them to identify him.

(*The grounded spears of* BICHRI, HETH *and* MEMU-CAN *are shaking.* BATH-SHEBA *observes them.*)

77

MOTHER OF THAT WISDOM

BATH-SHEBA

H'm! Through the door or *over the wall*. I wonder. Does Israel hold men who have learned to fly?

AZARIAH
(Kindly)

No, my lady.

BATH-SHEBA

Or to climb like lizards?

AZARIAH

Hardly, my lady.

BATH-SHEBA
(Close to the shaking and sweating trio of guards)
Are you men feeling ill?

BICHRI

F-fever, my lady!

BATH-SHEBA

Oh? I have heard that such ills can be cured by the removal of the head. . . . Come, children. (*She exits L.* ABISHAG *and* ITTAI *follow.*)

AZARIAH

Poor thing. So bewildered. You three! Report for physic! (*He exits R.*)

BICHRI

That's not what *I* need.

Curtain

ACT ONE

Scene II

THE SCENE   *A room in the pavilion of* BATH-SHEBA.
*It is a large chamber beamed and floored with cedar, its
walls covered with a light, clean plaster. It is comfort-
ably but conservatively furnished and hung.*

*It is evening of the same day. The room is well lighted
by mirrored lamps and an offstage sky, U, that holds
fading daylight.*

AT RISE   A group of six GIRLS sit on cushions on the
floor. *They sew on linen garments. They have more than
the average of good looks.*

NAAMAH, *mother of Rehoboam, sits on a chair near
the girl group. She sews on a garment of colored silk.*

*In a corner, UR, is a solid chair with arms, a foot
rest, and handles on the sides by which it can be carried.
In it sits* MAACAH, *the mother of the long dead Absalom,
son of David. She is a withered old woman with a broken
mind.*

The GIRLS *hum in minor harmony.*

BATH-SHEBA

(Staff in hand she enters vigorously L. ABISHAG,
bearing a foot-square wooden chest, follows her)

Dear, dear! Such running about! (*Dropping into a chair*) This palace would be twice as rewarding if it were half as generous. I *told* David he was sacrificing comfort for grandeur. But perhaps I'm putting on weight. (*Rising*) What do you think, dear? (*Turning in exhibition*) Be frank.

ABISHAG
(Peering)
No, my lady. From *no* profile. And the notches of your *belts* are evidence.

BATH-SHEBA
I suppose. Though it *is* a wonder: I eat like a breeding she-goat. (*Sitting*) Well, at any rate—there can be *no* doubt those girls will be mothers. In the closet for drugs, dear. (*Indicating box held by* ABISHAG) Wait. The oil. (*She takes bottle from box, pours oil on hands, starts rubbing it in,* ABISHAG *exiting* R.) Unless they are stoned. The rest of you must take it as a lesson. (*Rising*) Fold up your work now, it is getting late.

GIRL A
My lady, will the king not ever again—visit us?

BATH-SHEBA
(*To one of the* GIRLS)
Strike the gong, dear, my hands are gooey. (*To* GIRL A *as* GIRL *strikes gong*) Just keep hoping, child; in the meantime keep busy. And remember I depend upon you to keep the other girls cheerful. (*Two women enter to*

conduct GIRLS.) I shall see you here next week when it is your turn again. (*She exits R to wipe the oil from her hands,* GIRLS *exiting L.*)

REHOBOAM
(Pushing a toy chariot he races in)
Chariots! Out of the way! Chariots! Get in, Mother! You be the warrior and I shall be the horse!

NAAMAH
Wait, my son. (*She wipes his face*) You must not overtire yourself.

REHOBOAM
I never get tired. I'm strong! (*But he sits at her feet.* BATH-SHEBA *enters—pauses in doorway.*) Aren't I strong, Mother?

NAAMAH
Yes, my son. But even the strong must rest.

REHOBOAM
I'm very strong. . . . But Mother—

NAAMAH
Yes?

REHOBOAM
Sometimes I am frightened.

NAAMAH
Why, my son?

MOTHER OF THAT WISDOM

REHOBOAM

When my father dies, I shall be king . . .

NAAMAH

Yes?

REHOBOAM

But—suppose no one will obey me?

NAAMAH

Everyone must obey the king.

REHOBOAM

Yes! (*He jumps up*) They will *have* to obey me! (*He strides around*) I shall *make* them! I shall make *them* afraid!

BATH-SHEBA

No, grandson. (*Moving in*) Much better to make them love you.

REHOBOAM

Yes! (*striding*) They *must* love me! I shall *make* them! If they don't I shall—I shall *whip* them!

MAACAH

(*Tugs at* REHOBOAM'*s sleeve*)

Absalom!—

REHOBOAM

I'm not Absalom!

82

MOTHER OF THAT WISDOM

BATH-SHEBA

Soon, Maacah, soon.

MAACAH

Is there word?

REHOBOAM

Oh, Absalom is dead!

BATH-SHEBA

Hush!

MAACAH

Dead?

BATH-SHEBA

The dead, yes, your son has to bury them. It was a great battle. But he *will* be home soon.

MAACAH

Soon. Yes. Absalom!—

REHOBOAM

He is dead, isn't he, grandmother?

BATH-SHEBA
(Low, closing her eyes)
. . . Yes, dear.

REHOBOAM

I know. Grandfather David killed him.

BATH-SHEBA

No. . . . A soldier killed him. . . . Your grandfather loved him very much.

REHOBOAM

But Queen Tahpnes says Grandfather killed him! His own son!

BATH-SHEBA

Pah! . . . (*Then coldly but reasonably*) Do you know what your grandfather used to say, Rehoboam? "As a jewel of gold in a pig's nose, so is a fair woman that tells lies." And did you say "Queen" Tahpnes, dear?

REHOBOAM

Yes, the queen. She is the queen, isn't she?

BATH-SHEBA

Well, perhaps *a* queen. Queen Number Thirty-eight, shall we say?

NAAMAH

Rehoboam, I want you to stay away from the lady Tahpnes.

REHOBOAM

I shan't! Why?

NAAMAH

Because I ask you to.

84

MOTHER OF THAT WISDOM

REHOBOAM

Oh, you! You make me sick!

NAAMAH

My son—

REHOBOAM

I know. You want me to be just a stupid Jew! *She* told me! And sit around like a—like a *"dreary cow"* as you do, because you are jealous! *That's* what she said! Well, I shan't! I am going to have—pleasure! And you can't stop me!

(NAAMAH *lowers her head.* MAACAH *wails.* REHOBOAM's *eyes drop before* BATH-SHEBA's.)

BATH-SHEBA
(Low and slow)

Apologize to your mother, Rehoboam. (REHOBOAM *sulks. Abruptly* BATH-SHEBA *blazes, in startling transformation*) Apologize! At once!

REHOBOAM
(He quails)

. . . I am sorry.

BATH-SHEBA
(Relatively innocuous again)

Yes. . . . You must not say cruel things through ignorance. Better to say nothing—always—unless you *know* the truth of your words. Do you understand?

MOTHER OF THAT WISDOM

REHOBOAM

. . . Yes, Grandmother.

BATH-SHEBA

Remember. . . . (*She touches his head*) Now you had better go along and do some lessons. (ABISHAG *enters R.* MALE SERVANT *enters L.*)

MALE SERVANT

My lady, the king approaches.

BATH-SHEBA

Excellent! I was hoping he would come! (NAAMAH *rises to exit.*) No, Naamah. Let your pain breed pity, not hatred. (SOLOMON *enters L.* ITTAI *follows.*) Welcome, my son!

SOLOMON

My mother! *And* my son! *And* his *chariot!*

REHOBOAM

Yes, Father! Father, I do want a horse! A little one!

SOLOMON
(*He tousles his son's head*)
Little ones break little necks. (*He sees* NAAMAH) My lady Naamah!

NAAMAH
(*She bends her knee*)
My lord! (*She exits R.*)

MAACAH

Absalom!—

SOLOMON

Good news, Mother Maacah! He will be home tomorrow!

MAACAH

(As BATH-SHEBA *signals for servants)*
Home? My son?

SOLOMON

Most surely home. Peace to you now—sleep—rest—

MAACAH

*(Wailing softly as slaves lift her chair and exit L
with her)*
Absalom! . . . My son!—

SOLOMON

. . . If he had lived he would be king. And I should
be dead.

BATH-SHEBA
(Low)

Yes, my son.

REHOBOAM

Father, then a big horse! Please!

MOTHER OF THAT WISDOM

SOLOMON

Do not whine, Rehoboam, I am weary. Go along and amuse yourself. Why don't you visit the lady Tahpnes? (*He sits.*)

REHOBOAM

Thank you, Father. I should like that. (*He exits L, throwing an unpleasant look of triumph at* BATH-SHEBA.)

BATH-SHEBA

The boy should spend more time with *you*, my son.

SOLOMON

It is well that he learn the ways of foreigners.

BATH-SHEBA

But he needs *your* counsel. It is so vital that he have complete reverence for *our* ways, and traditions—

SOLOMON

Yes, Mama, yes—some other time. Ittai— (*He leans back*) The little song of the garden: Sing it.

ITTAI

(*He moves down, striking his lute,* ABISHAG *moves down—goes still, near him—as he sings*)
A garden enclosed is my sister, my spouse;
(*He is singing to* ABISHAG—*whose eyes are worshipfully on him.* SOLOMON's *eyes are on both of them, in languid observation.*)
A spring shut up, a fountain sealed.

88

Awake, O north wind, and come thou south!
Blow upon my garden!
Blow upon my garden!

SOLOMON

Very lovely. The song, I mean. (*To* ABISHAG) Lovely
—don't you think, my dear?

ABISHAG
(Eyes lowered)

Yes, my lord.

SOLOMON
(To ITTAI*)*

And such a lovely maiden to hear it. Don't you think,
Ittai?

ITTAI
(His head is down)

. . . My lord.

SOLOMON

Lovely. Have the scribes record it. (*His eyes close;
he sighs*) Now leave me for the moment.

(ITTAI *exits quickly L, leaving his lute.* ABISHAG,
touching the lute enroute, exits R.)

BATH-SHEBA
(Watching the languid SOLOMON*)*

. . . Solomon.

MOTHER OF THAT WISDOM

SOLOMON

Uh?

BATH-SHEBA

Stir yourself, my son. A riddle.

SOLOMON

Ah, yes, Mama: (*Dreamily*) A man and a woman are two? . . . Of course. . . . Till God makes them one.

BATH-SHEBA

You are dreaming, my son. Wake up, now. A *riddle*.

SOLOMON

Uh? . . . Say it, Mama.

BATH-SHEBA

What folly greater than to praise a balky beast?

SOLOMON

. . . To carry it.

BATH-SHEBA

To goad a resistant people.

SOLOMON

Pish! Man or beast, if he balks he must be driven.

BATH-SHEBA

Man's unwillingness to go, ever has a cause, my son. Remove the cause.

90

SOLOMON

Pah! (*Rousing*) Am I God that I can put brains into the empty heads of the men of Israel? The cause is stupidity!

BATH-SHEBA

My son—

SOLOMON

All that I do is for them! Temple, aqueduct, the host!—

BATH-SHEBA

Peace, my son; gently. The cause is haste. You strive to do in a lifetime the work of centuries.

SOLOMON

Certain pharaohs have done as much.

BATH-SHEBA

In Egypt—where men are born to slavery and the whip, where strength is never without cruelty. (SOLOMON *gestures*) Yes, my son! For the Jew, strength without justice is abomination, a mockery of Jehovah's laws.

SOLOMON
(A bit loftily)

The strong king knows only laws that fit his time and necessity.

BATH-SHEBA

Now, what a silly thing for her to say.

91

MOTHER OF THAT WISDOM

SOLOMON

Her?

BATH-SHEBA

Of course, it *sounds* impressive. But your father used to say, "Let the musical phrase make sense." You would not *really* annul The Commandments, would you?

SOLOMON

Who said anything about The Commandments?

BATH-SHEBA

I understood that Tahpnes had advised you to—

SOLOMON

Nothing of the kind! She advises only strength and discipline!

BATH-SHEBA

At the cost of chaos? Surely she strokes you with smoke, my son.

SOLOMON

No one strokes me with smoke! Why should she stroke me with smoke?

BATH-SHEBA

Well, your father used to say that when a—

SOLOMON

Oh, bother my father! Mama, I came here to relax and you heckle me!

MOTHER OF THAT WISDOM

BATH-SHEBA

No, my son. (*She touches his arm*) You came because your mind is heavy with problems. Speak of them.
. . . New taxes, higher prices, lower wages. How to make
it go, eh?

SOLOMON

It *must* go.

BATH-SHEBA

Oh, my dear boy, it can't go! It's unsound! Wait!
Your whole scheme is wrong. Neither man nor nation
can live beyond income. Don't answer now, just think
of what I say: how easy, really, it would be to start a
program of economy. No great change; it would take
little to bring a balance between expense and revenue.
Small but overall economies. And happy men do twice
the work of malcontents; study the way to make them
happy and you will need fewer; that will leave more on
the land to swell the revenues. And oh, my son, one important thing! That foreign evil, the whip! Wait! Think,
if tomorrow you would tell the people it was gone! Oh,
I do believe if *that* were gone—! (*She is weeping*) Don't
be displeased with me, my son! I do so want to help
you!— (*She chokes off.*)

SOLOMON

No, no, Mama! There, now. Peace, now. Never have
I been "displeased" with you. I only say you should not
think ill of Tahpnes.

93

MOTHER OF THAT WISDOM

BATH-SHEBA

I must stop this; it leaves my nose like a glowing coal.

SOLOMON

You don't understand her, Mama. She is a remarkable woman.

BATH-SHEBA

How, dear?

SOLOMON

Generally. Her mind, the things she says. She has the most unusual voice I have ever heard. You must have noticed.

BATH-SHEBA

I know what you mean.

SOLOMON

And you must believe *this,* Mama: that her only concern is my welfare. It hurts her, physically, that men laugh at me.

BATH-SHEBA

Laugh at you? *Who* laughs at you? *Why?*

SOLOMON

Men. Weakness amuses them.

BATH-SHEBA

What weakness?

MOTHER OF THAT WISDOM

SOLOMON

(He gestures)

That which led me to spare the life of Ahijah.

BATH-SHEBA

Now, by the Ark! To so miscall your *strength!* Does Israel butcher its prophets?

SOLOMON

He is a false prophet.

BATH-SHEBA

That is not for us to judge! . . . But return to your problems, my son. Galilee, King Hiram's demand.

SOLOMON

Yes. Hiram. . . . Can I give him Asher, Zebulon and Naphtali?

BATH-SHEBA

Not without revolution.

SOLOMON

Revolution could be put down.

BATH-SHEBA

The germ would live in a memory of horror. No.

SOLOMON

Then what? To live, Israel *must* import from Tyre!

BATH-SHEBA

The demand is unlike Hiram. This Ahuram, his emissary: I wonder.

SOLOMON

Why should he misrepresent?

BATH-SHEBA

I don't know. Well, you can do only what you *can* do, my son. Perhaps the offer of a small part of Asher. Surely Hiram will not refuse to bargain.

SOLOMON

U'm. I must think. (*He rises.*)

BATH-SHEBA
(Rising)

Solomon. . . . May I ask something? . . . (SOLOMON *waits, anticipating.*) Before morning you must make grave decisions. Will you make them alone?

SOLOMON

I told you. You are not fair to her.

BATH-SHEBA

Call it that, call it anything! But please, just tonight! One night! It is little to ask!

SOLOMON

All right, Mama, all right! I must go. (*He exits quickly L.* BATH-SHEBA *stands, sighs, shakes her head.*)

MOTHER OF THAT WISDOM

ITTAI

(He enters L)
Your pardon, my lady. My lute—

BATH-SHEBA

Of course, child. It was a beautiful song. (ABISHAG *enters R*) Won't you come again soon and sing for me?

ITTAI

I would be honored, my lady! Thank you! (*He exits with lute.*)

BATH-SHEBA

(She observes that ABISHAG's *eyes follow* ITTAI)
An attractive young man. (*Sitting*) And talented. Rub my back, dear. (ABISHAG *obeys.*) That is good. Backs just *were* made to be rubbed. . . . A musician has such good chances in Israel. Of course, this boy is not David, but he will probably marry the daughter of a lord. (ABISHAG *bursts into tears.*) There, there, dear, I know. You are in love, aren't you? Of course. You love the king and he spurns you.

ABISHAG

No! Oh, no!

BATH-SHEBA

How surprising. Because it could not be that you love that—now, what is his name, that lute player?

ABISHAG

. . . Ittai.

MOTHER OF THAT WISDOM

BATH-SHEBA

. . . You make it sound like a prayer—the *name* of love. I suppose all women do . . . David . . . (ITTAI *bolts in, pulls up*) Well! What sharp ears!

ITTAI

The king dismissed me, my lady, and—you said soon!

BATH-SHEBA

And what a literal mind! Well, as long as you are here you can help Abishag. She has something in her eyes. I must go see about anything. (*And as she exits R*) I shan't be gone *very* long.

ITTAI

(Kerchief in hand)

My lady—madam—I mean—could I—(ABISHAG *turns to him. With a moan he drops to his knee, kisses her hand*) Tell me I offend you and I will kill myself!

ABISHAG

Do not say such things. And do not kneel. (*She draws him up.*)

ITTAI

But I don't know what to do! Abishag, I love you, and—don't you see?

ABISHAG

Yes.

98

ITTAI

You mean you—you love *me?*

ABISHAG

Yes.

ITTAI

Oh, my darling! (*Going to his knee.*)

ABISHAG

You must not kneel. (*She draws him up*) I am the daughter of the poorest farmer in Shunam.

ITTAI

You are a prince's daughter! Oh, my love, you are so beautiful! Everyone sees it. The great men speak of it, and the soldiers! Even the queens and the concubines praise you!

ABISHAG

Please. No.

ITTAI

Then you do *not* love me!

ABISHAG

I do.

ITTAI

Then how can we go on living? You belong to the king!

99

ABISHAG

No! That is—I am a maid.

ITTAI

But *Solomon!* Still you are *his!*

ABISHAG

It is said in Shunam: "You can pay for the hand, you cannot pay for the heart."

ITTAI

Oh, my own! What can we do?

ABISHAG

Perhaps— I think the queen-mother knows.

ITTAI

But how could she? We just told each other!

ABISHAG

She seems to know everything. Do you mean you— want me to wed?

ITTAI

Of course! Oh, my dove, my love, my—! (*She goes into his arms and they kiss passionately.*)

BATH-SHEBA
(*Entering R*)

That's right, my dears, don't quarrel. (*The two go to their knees before her*) Jehovah give his blessing to you. Rise now. You love each other, eh? Well, I'm sure it is a very nice love, so I shall try to help you. (*The two go to their knees again as she strikes the gong*) Don't keep bobbing up and down. Of course, you will have to leave Israel for while. (*Servant enters*) Send to the chambers of Kinyras, the Wise Man of Tyre. Say that Queen Bath-Sheba requests his presence here this evening. Go. (*Servant exits*) But if you have each other, then nothing else matters much, does it?

ITTAI *and* ABISHAG

Nothing, my lady! My *lady!*

BATH-SHEBA

That is as it should be. Well, enough now, more later. Ittai: did the king go to his own pavilion?

ITTAI

Yes, my lady.

BATH-SHEBA

He goes often to that of the Egyptian woman, does he?

ITTAI

(*He is suddenly more than naturally discomposed*)
Every night, my lady.

BATH-SHEBA

. . . Yes. . . .

101

MOTHER OF THAT WISDOM

ITTAI

My lady! (*He goes to his knee*) There is a thing I know!

BATH-SHEBA

Yes?

ITTAI

I fear to speak of it!

BATH-SHEBA

Speak. Without fear.

ITTAI

Three days gone I bore a message to the lady Tahpnes! I came unannounced to an inner chamber! There I beheld the queen—disrobed—in the arms of a man! It was the lord Jeroboam!

BATH-SHEBA
(Her eyes widen)

Jeroboam!

ITTAI

He, my lady, I swear it!

BATH-SHEBA

So! That one! (*Her abrupt anger transforms her. It is startling as a sudden red lance of flame*) The slippery upstart who upholds her every destructive suggestion! A *conspiracy!*—I felt it, I *felt* it! *That* pair of Jehovah be-damned reptiles! Well!—this demands immediate investigation, my dear children! (*She belabors the gong*) Immediate! My son is *weak*, is he? *Men laugh at him, do they?* (*To* MALE SERVANT *who is one of four servants who enter hastily, three being women*) Go to Tahpnes, the Egyptian woman! Inform her that Queen Bath-Sheba will visit her within the hour! *Go!* (*To women, as* MALE SERVANT *exits*) I venture to visit a *whore* so bring me appropriate clothing! Wild-colored silks—a nasty broad sash for my bottom—sandals of crimson and—No! Wait! *White!*—that is it, *clean white linen!* I *visit* the brothel, not *enter* it! Turn your back, Ittai, and sing! *Exultantly!*

ITTAI
(*He strikes his lute loudly and sings* fortissimo—*as*
ABISHAG *begins* BATH-SHEBA'*s disrobing*)
Go forth, O ye daughters of Zion,
And behold King Solomon!
Behold him with the crown
Wherewith his mother crowned him!—

Curtain

ACT ONE

Scene III

THE SCENE   *The audience hall of Tahpnes' pavilion shortly following. The room is a transplanted bit of Egypt. Its architecture, decorations, furniture might be part of the pharaoh's palace. Upstage, C, concealed by sliding panels, is a pagan altar. On the floor, L and D, is a 4-foot replica of the crouching Giza Sphinx. It conceals a trapdoor that lifts from R to L, the figure tilting up with the door. A concealed bell connects with the floor passage.*

AT RISE   *The large square treasure baskets of Scene I lie at stage L. U and C* TAHPNES *reclines on a divan.* REHOBOAM *crouches on the floor beside her. Around them is a noisy group of Egyptian men and women who watch two dwarfs fight with truncheons.*

    DWARF A *strikes other on the foot—who squeals, leans to rub it.* TAHPNES *cuts him across his rear with a whip. The other dwarf screams,* DWARF A *dives for him, both tumble behind furniture and* DWARF A *clubs him "out."*

DWARF A
(Prostrating himself)
Reward, great lady, for the victor!

MOTHER OF THAT WISDOM

(Urged by TAHPNES, REHOBOAM *lashes the* DWARF, *who howls. Both dwarfs are dragged off by four joyous revelers.)*

REHOBOAM

I did it!

GROUP

He did!
He did!

TAHPNES
(She strokes his head)

He is becoming quite like an Egyptian. If it were not for that nose— (*The* GROUP *laughs.* REHOBOAM *hides his nose. Under* TAHPNES' *stare the* GROUP *silences.* (Is it kind to laugh at the boy's misfortune? There, dear. You must develop a character that will dispute your features.

REHOBOAM

How?

TAHPNES

Be strong; remembering that the people of Israel respect only scorn and the whip. (*A* SERVANT *enters L, goes to his knees*) Speak.

SERVANT

A person from the queen-mother, great lady, announcing her intention to call upon the princess—within the hour.

106

TAHPNES

Oh, yes—the trash. (*Indicating baskets*) Say that she has my permission.

(SERVANT *exits.*)

REHOBOAM

Now, why does *she* have to come?

TAHPNES

When people grow brain-simple, dear, one never knows what they will do.

(*The floor-passage bell jangles.*)

REHOBOAM

What is that?

TAHPNES

A prayer bell, dear. I must be alone. (*To* GROUP) Take the prince with you and amuse him.

(*A general exit leaves only* TAHPNES *and the servant* HATHOP *on stage. Under* HATHOP's *tug the Sphinx figure tilts up and back, taking the trapdoor with it.* AD'HOTEP, *holding a lamp, ascends to stage from concealed steps.* AHURAM, *the Tyrian, follows him.*)

AD'HOTEP

Ahuram, my lady, emissary of Tyre.

TAHPNES
(Coldly)

What do you want?

AHURAM

Gold. The balance due me.

TAHPNES

You get the gold when results prove you have done your work.

AHURAM

The results will be tomorrow's revolution. By which time the queen Tahpnes will be well on her way to Egypt.

AD'HOTEP

Careful, scum.

AHURAM

Scum, is it? Deliver the gold. Or shall I receive word from King Hiram that he has changed his mind regarding Galilee?

(At TAHPNES' *gesture* AD'HOTEP *lifts a bag of gold from a chest, sets it on table, exits R,* HATHOP *following.)*

TAHPNES

(She rises, approaches close to AHURAM*)*

The gold is there. . . . (AHURAM *takes her by the arms*) Will you take the gold?

AHURAM

The gold also. (*He draws her to him.*)

TAHPNES

No. (AHURAM *steps back hastily.* TAHPNES *has been holding the point of a dagger against his middle.* AD'HO-TEP, *with a lead-tipped whip, reenters.* HATHOP *follows*) Go with your gold.

AD'HOTEP
(To HATHOP*)*

See him down. Then bring the lord Benaiah.

(AHURAM *takes the gold, starts down the passage stairs, pauses, looks at* TAHPNES, *spits, descends.* AD'HOTEP'*s lash flashes down through the floor hole.* AHURAM *screams. . . .* HATHOP *descends with lamp.* AD'HOTEP *lowers trapdoor and figure into place.*)

TAHPNES

Jewish beast.

AD'HOTEP
(Sharply)

I would remind the princess that all Semites are not Jews!

TAHPNES

You are too sensitive, Ad'hotep.

AD'HOTEP

Edom too is Semitic! And my forebears were kings in Edom before the Jews ever heard of Israel!

109

MOTHER OF THAT WISDOM

TAHPNES
I never think of you as anything but an Egyptian.

AD'HOTEP
Sufficient if you think of me as an Edomite—who will one day rule not only Edom but Judah!—even *all* Israel!—*with* the promised blessing of your father, the pharaoh!

TAHPNES
And welcome, my friend. Praise Ra I shall be out of the cursed place before another day ends.

AD'HOTEP
That will depend on Solomon's decisions.

TAHPNES
I will arrange his decisions.

AD'HOTEP
But on all points! These Jews grumble readily but fundamentally they are patient. Only complete outrage will drive them to revolution.

TAHPNES
They will have it.

AD'HOTEP
May I warn the princess not to underestimate the sagacity of the queen-mother, Bath-sheba?

TAHPNES

Sagacity? That would be difficult. Oh, she is about to visit me!

AD'HOTEP

Now? But Benaiah, the group?—they are due.

TAHPNES

Not quite yet. I shall get rid of her quickly. You have completed arrangements for our flight?

AD'HOTEP

Ten chariots wait at this moment—and relays to the border—thanks to the "noble" lord Jeroboam.

TAHPNES

Ah, yes—Jeroboam. I look forward to his position in Egypt—under my foot.

AD'HOTEP

You will miss that pleasure. He now plans to flee north, to Asher, to await Ahijah's call. Which reminds me, I must go and fetch the worthy prophet.

TAHPNES

You are not bringing *him* here?

AD'HOTEP

Since he is the key piece in our game—

111

MOTHER OF THAT WISDOM

TAHPNES

I won't have it! You will manage otherwise!

AD'HOTEP

(Sharply)

May I remind the princess that the pharaoh ordered her to obey me?

TAHPNES

My father has never smelled an unwashed lunatic!— (SERVANT *enters L, goes to his knees*) Speak!

SERVANT

Bath-sheba the queen-mother, great lady!

TAHPNES

When .you hear the gong. First bring the boy. (SERVANT *exits R.*) You must realize *all* this political skulduggery is extremely boring to me.

AD'HOTEP

Patience. Only hours now and you will be free of it. (*By exit portal L*) With this one:—(*Indicating offstage* BATH-SHEBA) be cunning. (*Exiting L.*)

REHOBOAM

(Entering R with SERVANT, *who exits L, he finds a reclining and deeply saddened* TAHPNES)
Oh! What is it? (*Dropping to the floor beside her.*)

TAHPNES

Dear Rehoboam. (*Drawing him to her*) Only you have been kind to me. Will you always remember that Tahpnes loved you?

REHOBOAM

Oh, yes! But what is wrong?

TAHPNES

(She strikes the gong)

Your grandmother is here. Always remember. (BATH-SHEBA *enters, her anger now covered by varying degrees of zanyism.* ABISHAG *follows.*) My lady Bath-sheba!

BATH-SHEBA

(Her reaction to the divan scene is almost
perfectly restrained)

My lady Tahpnes! . . . You will go to your quarters, Rehoboam.

TAHPNES

Go, dear. (*She kisses him.*)

REHOBOAM

(He walks stiffly to exit L, turns)

If you are unkind to her I shall—I shall put you to the sword! (*He exits.*)

TAHPNES

(Laughing gently)

Such a dear little champion.

113

MOTHER OF THAT WISDOM

BATH-SHEBA

(Contemplating the staff in her hand)

This was his grandfather David's staff. Perhaps I should give it to him—on his bottom. (*She drops dull care, beams about her*) How snug! Oh, yes, here are the baskets! You have taken what you need?

TAHPNES

Nothing. I want you to have it all.

BATH-SHEBA

Why, how kind! (*Fingering the silks*) This will delight the girls. (*To* ABISHAG) Feel, dear. . . . And the drugs and spices?

TAHPNES

I will have everything carried to your pavilion.

BATH-SHEBA

You *are* kind. Shall I sit here? (*As she sits beside* TAHPNES) I have very good feet but I do ask a lot of them. And my husband used to say, "Death looks for one with cranky feet." That is why I tell Solomon to pamper his feet. Though heaven knows, no one could be better at dodging death.

TAHPNES

He has had to dodge it?

BATH-SHEBA

Even before he was born! And it is so silly of them; his enemies—they all just die.

TAHPNES

How remarkable.

BATH-SHEBA

Oh, he is! Do you know, he even felt like a king before he was born. But I must not bore you with baby stories.

TAHPNES

Oh, I am terribly interested!

BATH-SHEBA

Now you are stroking *me* with smoke. But you are right, there is no fool like a doting mother. Unless it might be a treacherous wife; that is, in Israel. We throw large stones at them.

TAHPNES

If you catch them.

BATH-SHEBA

Oh, we catch them! Jehovah gave us the world's finest nose for smelling out sin.

TAHPNES

Then *that* is what it is for.

MOTHER OF THAT WISDOM

BATH-SHEBA
Eh? Oh, yes! Mankind will never be free of sin till everyone wears a Jewish nose.

TAHPNES
(She laughs)
You Jews: with your self-importance. Don't you know you are the laughingstock of the world?

BATH-SHEBA
Are they so afraid of us?

TAHPNES
Afraid? (*She is beginning really to feel the sharpness of the needle.*)

BATH-SHEBA
But I suppose they know we have been chosen.

TAHPNES
By Ra, you *are* a treasure! Chosen, yes! For extinction!

BATH-SHEBA
For immortality. Oh, yes! To live and rule when all other peoples have become only dust.

TAHPNES
(She snorts)
Then *Israel* will outlive *Egypt?*

BATH-SHEBA

Egypt? My dear— (*So kindly*) there will be a Jewish nation when Egypt is remembered only because she pickled *people*.

TAHPNES

You insulting bag of— Why, your filthy little kingdom is collapsing under you even as you sit there!

BATH-SHEBA

But you must not be offended! We all hope Egypt will hang on for quite a *long* while! I tell Solomon he should help her!

TAHPNES

Very decent! But slightly impossible! Since by this time tomorrow you will both be dead!

BATH-SHEBA

Beg pardon?

TAHPNES

I don't mind your knowing! Tell him! He will laugh at you!

BATH-SHEBA

My dear child, you *are* overwrought! There now, I assure you, I have the highest opinion of Egypt! Though I do wish the pharaohs would not marry their own mothers.

117

MOTHER OF THAT WISDOM

TAHPNES

Sisters!

BATH-SHEBA

Sisters. There is something not quite nice about it.

TAHPNES

There was something quite *nice,* was there, about the murder of your first husband?

BATH-SHEBA

Uriah?

TAHPNES

Uriah. The noble David lusts for a married female and has her husband slaughtered. Quite nice?

BATH-SHEBA

Quite untrue. David was not guilty of Uriah's death. . . . (TAHPNES *sneers*) I was. (TAHPNES *reacts.* BATH-SHEBA *continues, and now, subtly, she has changed, and there is nothing of the fool in her somberly quiet and sincerely reminiscent words, words spoken as though to herself, or to a sympathetic friend*) I was fourteen when they sold me to him. He was fifty-two. He was a Hittite: he worshipped a little golden image. Because I persistently acknowledged Jehovah he whipped me—whipped the body that was made to comfort a king, and bear a king. I paid for his death with the gold of the little image.

MOTHER OF THAT WISDOM

TAHPNES

. . . What a pretty tale for the gossips of Israel.

BATH-SHEBA

No one knows it. Not even David knew. (*She rises*)
Of course, *you* could tell it. But who would believe an
Egyptian?—even in Egypt. (*To* ABISHAG) Come, dear.
(*She exits L, leaving her staff.* ABISHAG *follows.*)

TAHPNES

(*In fury she leaps from the divan. She sees the staff,
picks it up, strikes the gong*)
Bok! (*A large Nubian mute enters, prostrates himself. She thrusts the staff at him*) Break it! (*The mute
tries, fails. She snatches up her whip*) Break it!

(*The mute makes a frantic effort, fails. He casts the
staff away, drops to the floor. With throat noises
and whining he crawls backwards to exit R and
through it.* TAHPNES *follows him. The impact of the
lash is heard, and the howl of the mute. They are
repeated. Moaning, the mute scrambles crablike to
the stage. The whip is thrown after him. . . . He
recovers and sits, rubbing his back. The floor-
passage bell sounds. He ignores it.*)

ABISHAG

(*She enters hurriedly, looks around*)
Staff? The queen-mother's staff!

119

(The mute grins, opens his tongueless mouth, points to it. Searching, ABISHAG *finds the staff as the mute, after a leisurely rising and crossing, tilts up the sphinx figure. As the floor passage opens* ABISHAG *is positioned behind a basket with a raised lid. A Caucasian slave ascends with a lamp.* JEROBOAM *follows. As the slave exits into floor passage* ABISHAG *steps into the basket, lowers the lid. The mute lowers the floor door.)*

JEROBOAM

The princess. *(The mute exits.* JEROBOAM *pours and drinks wine.* TAHPNES *enters)* My darling! *(* JEROBOAM *starts to embrace her.)*

TAHPNES
(Arching back from him)
Is that really necessary any longer?

JEROBOAM
(He steps back)
Perhaps not— *(Picking up his wine cup)* praise Baal.

TAHPNES
(She laughs)
The *wisely* wicked man is never a boor, my friend.
. . . Ad'hotep says you have decided to flee north.

JEROBOAM

Upon the advice of Ahijah. By the prophecy I am to rule over northern Israel alone, not Judah. He bids me be at hand.

120

TAHPNES

Prophecy! The man is moonstruck.

JEROBOAM
(He shrugs)

If it works—?

TAHPNES

I can't see you as king of anything. You are a child.

JEROBOAM

I am two years older than Solomon. (*Drinking.*)

TAHPNES

You compare yourself with Solomon?

JEROBOAM

Why not?

TAHPNES

The man is a king.

JEROBOAM

I thought you did not care for him.

TAHPNES

I hate him. (*She kicks the whip from her path.*
JEROBOAM *picks it up.*) He is five parts fool and all Jew.
But he does have stature; an honest *desire* to rule effec-
tively. With a touch of hard wisdom he would be dangerous—and a less effective lover.

121

JEROBOAM

Interesting. And what am I?

TAHPNES

You? The very worst type of Jew. And let me say now, in secret confession, that apart from my cultivated prejudice, and my, *yes, limited* perspicacity, I am not without awareness of the regrettable merits of Jews—*some* of them. They do have a strange tenacity, annoying dignity and ridiculously boundless ambition!—and an incomprehensible devotion to their impossible single god! (*She is pacing*) Even that obnoxious Captain Benaiah: He infuriates me. He is crude as a rutting goat, vulgar as a public belch, but he is a *man,* a Jew for Jews!—and a deplorably effective military leader. Oh, yes—I *would* be a fool to see otherwise. In fact, I could devoutly wish that the brute were Egyptian, performing in the service of my father. (*She ceases to pace, facing* JEROBOAM) Yes. There *are* Jews of regrettable merit. But you! You are a shallow cipher. You believe in nothing; you are without loyalty; you have no honesty. *And* you are a pretentious failure—in bed.

JEROBOAM

(*Through his teeth, as he fingers the whip*)
. . . And you are the queen—of strumpets.

TAHPNES

And that:—(*Indicating the whip*) You may yet need Egyptian refuge. Raise an insolent eyebrow within her borders and I will kill you with it.

122

JEROBOAM

(He bows—though white as lard)

I have *more* than a touch of hard wisdom, great lady. And your opinion be damned. (*The passage bell sounds.* JEROBOAM, *after a moment for recovery, lifts the Sphinx and trapdoor.* HATHOP *ascends with a lamp.* BENAIAH *ascends followed by* AZARIAH. HATHOP *closes floor door, exits R.*) My lord Benaiah! The captain Azariah!

TAHPNES

My lord Benaiah! (BENAIAH *nods.*)

JEROBOAM

You have before seen the captain Azariah, my lady?

TAHPNES

Yes. The captain has always pretended not to see me.

AZARIAH

No, my lady! That is— I, uh—

TAHPNES

Be comforted, captain. Studied refusal to notice a woman is the greatest compliment a man can pay her.

BENAIAH

Must we listen to whores' talk?

TAHPNES

And vulgar words have no meaning in the mouth of a vulgar man.

123

BENAIAH

Vulgar my ass! We are dogs and we despise each other! Where is the Shilonite?

JEROBOAM

Ad'hotep will bring him.

BENAIAH

This place stinks like an Amalekite harem tent. The lad here has thrown in with me. Don't bother to congratulate him. (*He observes route of tunnel passage*) How did you build this, that Solomon knew nothing of it?

JEROBOAM

Workers from Egypt, minus their tongues.

BENAIAH

A nice piece of work.

TAHPNES

You have heard of Egyptian engineers, my lord?

JEROBOAM

Oh, the lord Benaiah, too, has built an escape passage!

TAHPNES

Oh?

JEROBOAM

From the king's pavilion. Not more than ten thousand souls know of it.

BENAIAH

It was not planned as a way in for jackals. Regarding escape: *(To both)* You have arranged yours?

TAHPNES

We have, my lord.

BENAIAH

You start when?

JEROBOAM

Tonight, when the king has left the lady Tahpnes.

BENAIAH
(To Jeroboam)

You go to Egypt?

JEROBOAM

To the north. Ahijah feels that since—

BENAIAH

Yes, yes. *(To* TAHPNES*)* How do you know Solomon will visit you tonight?

TAHPNES

You embarrass me, my lord.

BENAIAH

Don't trifle! He must be led to decide as we have planned!

TAHPNES

He will visit me, my lord. He will decide exactly as we have planned.

BENAIAH

The fool. Is this your baggage? (*He indicates baskets*)
It is too much.

TAHPNES

I take nothing (*She strikes gong*) That is the goods
from the ships. (SERVANT *enters*) Remove this trash.
Then carry it to the queen mother.

> (*The passage bell sounds.* JEROBOAM *raises trap-
> door.* AD'HOTEP *ascends with a lamp.* AHIJAH *fol-
> lows. Slaves enter L, carry off baskets during im-
> mediately following dialogue.*)

JEROBOAM
(Goes to his knee)

O prophet of God!

AHIJAH

His favor continue with you! (*He gazes around in dis-
gust.*)

BENAIAH

Don't bother to look, old papa, just sniff.

JEROBOAM

Will you sit, Holy Man?

BENAIAH

We can do without ceremony. When does the revolt
break? Where? In what manner?

> (*Slaves exit with basket holding* ABISHAG.)

126

MOTHER OF THAT WISDOM

AHIJAH

Solomon will perform as we have planned?

JEROBOAM

He will, rabbi.

AHIJAH

Then at high noon the people will gather before the palace. Agitators will mingle with them to inflame them. Certain Galilean zealots will attain audience with Solomon, whom they will vilify. He will slay them. The people will rise and destroy the city.

BENAIAH

(To AZARIAH*)*

The earmark of certain holiness, you see: to speak of a city's death as you would the milking of a goat. *(To Ahijah)* And the host? We withdraw the host?

AHIJAH

Solomon will order an attack with whips. You will attack with the sword.

BENAIAH

Will we, now!

AHIJAH

You will slay without mercy, crazing the people. Then you will withdraw.

BENAIAH

By Abraham! I? Butcher my own people?

AHIJAH

Many must die that all may live in God!

AZARIAH

Slay them yourself then! I kill no Jews!

BENAIAH

Peace, lad. (*To* AHIJAH) We attack with fist and spear butt. Nothing more.

AD'HOTEP

Israelite captains are more willing to destroy the helpless of other lands.

BENAIAH
(He regards him)
Ah, yes!—"Ad'hotep." You speak for Egypt?

AD'HOTEP

For *Edom!* And not "Ad'hotep" but *Hadad!*—that prince of Edom whose every kin was slain by David and the butcher Joab!

BENAIAH

Well! One of those, eh?

AD'HOTEP

One of those! And a king! I!

BENAIAH

Perhaps. But for *my* sword a heathen troublemaker.

128

MOTHER OF THAT WISDOM

AD'HOTEP

Baal curse your sword, you circumcised dog!

AHIJAH

And Jehovah curse the tongue that calls on a false god! (*He raises his staff to strike* AD'HOTEP.)

BENAIAH
(*Thrusting* AHIJAH *back*)
False god, false prophet, Satan take both of them!

(JEROBOAM *draws his sword against* BENAIAH. AZA-RIAH *draws against* JEROBOAM.)

TAHPNES
(*She bursts into laughter*)
That's right, *rend* each other! Let us have *fools'* blood! (*Then viciously exultant*) Pah! What abysmal idiots you are, you Semites! One blood in all of you, one arrogant dream!—power and domination!—to be obtained through *liberty* and held by *peace!* And only union needed to force your lunacy on the world! Yes, from Babylon to the Nile! And do you find union? Never! Tribe against tribe, priest against priest, god against god, you squabble like birds over imaginary morsels! And so you have always done! And so you will always *do,* praise Ra, till Semites fly and the birds speak Hebrew! Now, go! (*Striking the gong*) Get out! And may I never again look upon your faces!

(HATHOP *enters with lamp.*)

MOTHER OF THAT WISDOM

BENAIAH
(To others, who stand silent)
Well? Shall we tear ourselves away, my fellow birds?

(HATHOP lifts passage door.)

AHIJAH
(He approaches a step toward TAHPNES)
Jehovah's curse upon you and yours till the end of
time!

*(He strides to floor passage, descends following
HATHOP. JEROBOAM bends his knee briefly to
TAHPNES, descends. AZARIAH follows.)*

BENAIAH
*(He descends three steps, pauses,
regards a rigid TAHPNES)*
Talking birds and flying Semites. *(He chuckles)* In
Canaan we have ravens that speak excellent Hebrew.
And already our angels fly. *(He descends, chuckling.)*

(AD'HOTEP slams the floor door, spits.)

TAHPNES
And you also! Get out of my sight! *(She strikes the
gong twice as AD'HOTEP, with a curt bow, exits stiffly R.
Several servants and slaves enter R and L)* I would worship! *(She reclines on the divan.)*

130

MOTHER OF THAT WISDOM

(Rapidly the chamber is prepared for "worship." The upstage wall panels are opened revealing the altar. It holds a life-sized image of Hathor, goddess of love and mirth. Subtly obscene, the semi-nude figure squats on swollen haunches, its right arm raised and crossed to press itself into exaggerated breasts, the hand holding a staff. Its head is that of a horned cow. Lamps throw reflected colored light on it. Incense pots are lighted. Musicians enter and make sensuous minor music on stringed instruments as TAHPNES *glides to the shrine and prostrates herself on a rug of padded silk. Slaves, male and female, squatting, chant softly and sway gently to the music. . . .* TAHPNES *turns—stretches out on her back. A large and muscular Caucasian slave crawls to her. . . . She strokes his head. . . . A* SERVANT *enters breathlessly L.)*

SERVANT

Great lady! The king approaches!

TAHPNES

(Rising in a fury)

Osiris *damn* the fool! Repair the chamber! Speed or die!

(In seconds the chamber is "repaired." Slaves and servants exit swiftly. TAHPNES *reclines on the divan.* SOLOMON *enters, pauses, crosses to her eagerly, kneels.)*

MOTHER OF THAT WISDOM

TAHPNES
(Pretending to awaken she opens her arms)
My beloved! (SOLOMON *enfolds her.*)

Curtain

ACT TWO

ACT TWO

ACT TWO

SCENE I

THE SCENE   BATHSHEBA's *pavilion, immediately following.*

The room is the same as in Act One, Scene II, except for the treasure baskets which stand in a corner. The lid of the basket in which ABISHAG *rode is open.*

AT RISE   BATH-SHEBA *and* ABISHAG *are on stage.* ABISHAG *has finished the story of what she has overheard.* BATH-SHEBA *is stunned and incredulous.*

BATH-SHEBA
I—I can't believe it! It seems impossible!

ABISHAG
My lady, I was *there,* in the *basket!* And I *heard,* and *saw!*

BATH-SHEBA
. . . But *Benaiah!* You could *not* be *wrong,* dear?

ABISHAG
(Pitying)
Oh, my lady—no—it was he.

BATH-SHEBA
(She is weeping)

I would sooner have believed that—But I must not go on like *this*. I must think. . . . *(Mastering her emotion)* Yes. . . . When and how will they strike? If only they had left you there long enough to learn that. Oh, my staff! But of course, you were not— *(But* ABISHAG *has popped to the basket. She pulls out the staff)* Oh, thank you, thank you! *(Taking it eagerly)* I feel really incapable without it. Now, let me see. The woman's words to *me*: that I would be dead by this time tomorrow. Oh, and that Azariah! He is such a likable young booby. When I think of Benaiah corrupting him— *(Thoughtfully)* He is a booby, don't you think, dear?

ABISHAG
(She giggles)

Yes, my lady.

BATH-SHEBA

Yes. Always the picture of dull sincerity, furiously loyal to something he does not understand—

ITTAI
(He enters quickly, goes to his knee)
My lady, the king has gone to the lady Tahpnes.

BATH-SHEBA
(She sighs)

Of course. I am afraid we have larger problems now, Ittai. (NAAMAH enters) Yes, Naamah?

MOTHER OF THAT WISDOM

NAAMAH

Those three girls are here, my mother. They beg
audience. They are quite pitiful.

BATH-SHEBA

Oh, not now, Naamah! Tell them I will— (*She stops,
stands tensely in thought*) Ittai! Quickly! The captain
Azariah, he will be leaving the palace! Find him, stop
him, tell him to report here immediately by order of the
king! (*And as* ITTAI *runs*) But alone, see him alone! Let
no one know! Speed! (ITTAI *exits.*) There! Now! Send
the girls in, Naamah. (NAAMAH *exits.*) The weak link,
dear, there is always a weak link. Jehovah grant we can
exploit it.

(*The three* GIRLS *enter. Each is lovely but somewhat
the worse for grief and fear.*)

GIRLS
(*Sobbing, they drop to their knees*)
Mercy, great lady, help us!
Great lady help us! We are to be stoned!
We are afraid, great lady! We are to be slain!

BATH-SHEBA

Hush, now, hush. And rise. Of course I will help you.

GIRLS
(*Kissing her hands*)
Oh, bless you, bless you, great lady!
Oh, thank you, great lady!
Jehovah bless you, great lady!

137

MOTHER OF THAT WISDOM

BATH-SHEBA

Stop it, now, hush, you sillies!—slobbering all over my hands. And rise! (*The* GIRLS *obey.*) Now, listen to me. I will help you, but you will have to help *me*—do just as I say. Do you understand?

GIRLS

Yes, great lady!

BATH-SHEBA

Very well. A man is coming here shortly, a soldier. He is the man who seduced you. You will know him by the scar on his face.

GIRL 1

Scar?

GIRL 2

But he *had* no—(*She stops.*)

BATH-SHEBA

Oh? Had he not?

GIRL 2

. . . Perhaps he had.

GIRL 3

Oh, yes! A scar!

BATH-SHEBA

Indeed, yes! A wonderful scar! Now, you are to go

in there. (*Gesturing R*) When he is here, Abishag will bring you out, and when you see him you will scream— not too loudly—and say: "It is he, it is he!" And: "The scar, the scar!" And: "That is the man, the father of our unborn babes!" Can you do that?

GIRL 2

Yes, great lady!

GIRL 3

"It is he, it is he!"

GIRL 1

"The scar, scar!"—

BATH-SHEBA

Yes, dears, but do your rehearsing in *there,* quietly. And if you perform nicely I promise I will manage your escape to a far land and a new life.

GIRLS

Oh, great lady!—
Oh, bless you, great lady!—
Great lady, bless you!—

BATH-SHEBA

And do *not* start *that* again. You can express your gratitude by a heart-wringing performance— (ITTAI *enters hastily, pausing at sight of girls*) Ittai, I *told* you to—

139

MOTHER OF THAT WISDOM

ITTAI

He is here, my lady! He was just below, leaving the chambers of the lord Benaiah!

BATH-SHEBA

Oh! Splendid! You see, Jehovah *is* with us! Go now, girls! Take them, Abishag! When you hear me clap, bring them in quickly! (*To* ITTAI, *as* ABISHAG *and* GIRLS *exit R*) Fetch him, Ittai; and tarry outside. Wait! (*She moves to a large chair, sits*) I shall be sitting here. A *monument* of indignation. (*She becomes the "monument"*) Now fetch him. (ITTAI *exits*) A *stuffy* monument. . . .

(ITTAI *enters with* AZARIAH—*who is in a sweat of fear.* ITTAI *exits.*)

AZARIAH

(*He glances around quickly in search of* SOLOMON, *goes to his knee before* BATH-SHEBA)
My lady!

BATH-SHEBA

The captain Azariah! . . . (*She stares down at him with "dreadful" severity*) The king is not here—as yet! . . . (*She watches him simmer*) Captain Azariah, your guilt is discovered! . . . Rise! . . . (AZARIAH *obeys, dread freezing him*) The girls have confessed!

AZARIAH

. . . Girls?

BATH-SHEBA

How contemptible of you. The king's own concubines!

AZARIAH

I do not understand, my lady.

BATH-SHEBA

Denials are useless! Their description identifies you as their seducer!

AZARIAH
(He is recovering rapidly, he draws himself up proudly)
There is a mistake, my lady.

BATH-SHEBA

A mistake? We shall see! (*She claps*) Miserable man!

GIRLS
(Herded in by ABISHAG. *They halt—stare—scream)*
It is he, it is he!
The scar, the scar! That is the man!
Yes! The father of our unborn babes!
*(*BATH-SHEBA *gestures. Still performing, ad libitum, the* GIRLS *are herded out by* ABISHAG.*)*

BATH-SHEBA

Miserable man!

AZARIAH
(He is mightily indignant)
This is an outrage, my lady! I am completely innocent!

141

BATH-SHEBA

Innocent?

AZARIAH

Innocent!

BATH-SHEBA

But only you could have attained access to the harem.

AZARIAH

I can only say, my lady, that I am not that kind of a man!

BATH-SHEBA
(Doubt seems to take her)

Dear me! Of course, it does seem odd, and I *would* like to believe you, but— Well, see: I shall ask you a few questions. Will you swear by the Holy Ark and in the name of Jehovah to answer?—speaking the truth and all of the truth?

AZARIAH

Gladly.

BATH-SHEBA

Swear.

AZARIAH

By the Holy Ark and in the name of Jehovah I swear to speak the truth!

142

MOTHER OF THAT WISDOM

BATH-SHEBA
(She rises. She continues to speak quietly, but her voice and eyes have become cold and hard)
The queen Tahpnes, the man Ad'hotep, the lord Jeroboam, the prophet Ahijah, the captain Benaiah and yourself conspire to bring about revolution and the death of the king. In *full*, what are the details of the conspiracy? Fulfill your oath. . . . (AZARIAH *is staring in terror. He draws back.* BATH-SHEBA *blazes) Fulfill your oath! Or Jehovah do thus and more to me if I do not have you slain and your body thrown to the dogs within the hour!* (AZARIAH *breaks. Sickened, he staggers)* Sit! . . . (AZARIAH *sags into chair)* The plot matures tomorrow. At what time of day? *Speak!*

AZARIAH
(He goes dull)
. . . Following the noon meal.

BATH-SHEBA
Yes. With Ahijah leading, the people will rise. And the City Host: you will withdraw the host? . . . *Speak!*

AZARIAH
The host will attack.

BATH-SHEBA
Attack the people?

AZARIAH
To craze them—before withdrawing.

143

MOTHER OF THAT WISDOM

BATH-SHEBA

Yes. . . . And Jeroboam: what is his gain?

(The curtain starts slowly down.)

AZARIAH

The crown—the prophet gives him the crown—at the bidding of Jehovah. He rules over all but Judah. Judah falls to Edom, at the pharaoh's pleasure—

Curtain

ACT TWO

SCENE II

THE SCENE   A room in the palace apartment of JERO-
BOAM. *The decorations betray an attempt at splendor by
use of the worst in Egyptian, Phoenician and Hebrew
furnishings.*

AT RISE   *It is an hour later.* JEROBOAM *is discovered
lolling on a divan. He is surrounded by* THREE YOUNG
FOLLOWERS *seated on floor cushions, and* TIKVAH *who is
sprawled in a chair.* LITTLE BOO, *a young harlot, lounges
on the divan beside* JEROBOAM. *All are quite drunk,*
JEROBOAM *and* TIKVAH *in particular.*

JEROBOAM
(His speech is slurred and slow)
—It cannot be dispuded, my frien's. Life is pleasure.
Therefore all that is not pleasure is death.

FOLLOWERS
T'hell with death!
We spit on it!
T'hell with it!

TIKVAH
S'nasty word!

145

JEROBOAM

Do nod interrup'. An' pleasure, my frien's, is a *re-clining* thing. Kingship, feasting, an' drinking: reclining things.

LITTLE BOO

An' love!

JEROBOAM

Do nod interrup'. Kingship is to recline an' order death for—for mos' anyone—while feasting an' drinking—while reclining.

LITTLE BOO

An' love!

JEROBOAM

Exac'ly. Love. Love is the *mos'* reclining thing. In any other than a reclining position love is very, very silly. An' so, my frien's, let us drain a cup to—to reclinatude.

LITTLE BOO

An' love!

(All drink.)

JEROBOAM
(He eyes LITTLE BOO *blearily)*

Oh, yes—Liddle Boo—Jerus'lem's leading author'dy on love—having practiced it until she wears it as a goat wears its odor. *How* could one not love her?

(All laugh.)

LITTLE BOO
(Slurring tipsily)

He does, he loves me! Tell them, Jerobobo! An' when you are king I sh'll be your fav'rite concubine, won't I?

TIKVAH

Liddle Boo, Liddle Boo! Harem lady ninedy-two! (*The men laugh.* TIKVAH *staggers from the chair*) The Gran' Prefec'! Tell them again, Jeroboam! Who is to be your Gran' Prefec'!

JEROBOAM

Tikvah, my good frien' Tikvah!

TIKVAH

The Gran' Prefec'! By Baal, I am grateful to you, Jerobobo!

JEROBOAM

All my frien's, my good frien's, you will be aroun' me!

FOLLOWERS

We are all grateful to you, my lord!
To our king!
Yes, to our king!

TIKVAH
(Draining his cup)

Jerobobo, king of Isra'l!

147

JEROBOAM
(He giggles)
Ahijah. That is the man for your graditude.

TIKVAH
Baal bless him, the good ol' soul, good ol' prophet!

JEROBOAM
Unexpected. *(Mumbling, partly to himself)* Never thoughd of such a thing. Slashed it into twelve pieces, the cloak. Mad, I said, he is mad. King of Isra'l, he said— King of Isra'l. *(He wags his finger)* But not Judah.

TIKVAH
In the dung-pit with Judah! Who wan's Judah?

FOLLOWERS
(They have quieted)
Peace, Tikvah.
Gently.

JEROBOAM
But Benaiah. Benaiah dies.

TIKVAH
Like a dog, the scoun'rel!

JEROBOAM
Mus' find another captain—to slay Benaiah—as he slew Joab. Jeroboamic justice. . . . Benaiah. . . . *(He laughs)* A riddle, a riddle!

148

FOLLOWERS

Say it!
Speak it!

JEROBOAM

What is dark an' sour as a hill of dung, an' stiff as a corpse in going?

FOLLOWERS

Benaiah!
Yes, Benaiah! (*Laughter.*)

JEROBOAM

Correc'!

TIKVAH

A riddle, a riddle!

JEROBOAM

Say it.

TIKVAH
(He has to enunciate carefully)
What, with countenance of a silly sheep, carries on its head a brush of rusty fire?

FOLLOWER

. . . A harlot in heat! Like this one! *(Slapping* LITTLE BOO's *bottom.*)

TIKVAH

Wrong!

149

LITTLE BOO

Do nod do that! I am his! Tell him, Jerobobo!

JEROBOAM

Hush. . . . (*Pondering*) "—countenance of a silly sheep—"

(The door R opens. ITTAI *enters, steps aside.* BATH-SHEBA *enters. She wears dark robes. She drops a fold of the dark covering that has been drawn over her head and face.* JEROBOAM *staggers to his feet, dumping* LITTLE BOO.*)*

TIKVAH

Bless Baal, the queen-mama! Oh, we should go!

JEROBOAM

Go? (*He sways*) Stay! (*He bows*) Unexpected pleasure, Queen-Mama. My frien's, kin'ly assume expressions of pleasure.

TIKVAH

(Hiding behind JEROBOAM *he tugs at his robe)*
When I become sober this will frighten me.

JEROBOAM

Frighten? Hush. No sush word.

BATH-SHEBA

The word is *fear*. (*Hard—still*) You think to build a barrier of wine between yourself and fear, Jeroboam?

JEROBOAM
(He giggles)
There is something *I* should fear?

BATH-SHEBA
Death.

JEROBOAM
(He laughs)
The dying smell death an' think the world is dying.
(He peers around for his guests who, all but TIKVAH,
have retreated to far corners) Where is everyone?

TIKVAH
(Behind him)
I am here.

JEROBOAM
So you are! Make yourself comf'table. *(To* BATH-
SHEBA) You were saying, funny lady? I seem to have los'
the thread.

BATH-SHEBA
The thread and your life. I came to plead with you,
Jeroboam, to remind you that all you have and are you
owe to my son. Instead I shall warn you: King Solomon
will not be torn from the throne by a craven sot.

JEROBOAM
. . . So you know.

BATH-SHEBA

Where will you flee, Jeroboam? To the west is the sea, to the east the desert, and there is no sanctuary to the north.

JEROBOAM

A riddle. East, west, north. To the south!

BATH-SHEBA

Yes. A renegade Jew in Egypt, living on his knees, inhaling with every breath the stink of his soul as it rots. Better be dead in Israel, Jeroboam.

JEROBOAM

Or king. You are nicer when you are stupid an' silly, Queen-Mama. (*He bursts into laughter, points at her*) Tikvah! "Countenance of a silly sheep, head a brush of rusty fire!" The queen-mama?

TIKVAH

Correc'! (*Staggering out hooting*) The queen-mama!

(*The* FOLLOWERS *and* LITTLE BOO *move out, taken by the contagion of drunken laughter.*)

JEROBOAM, TIKVAH, FOLLOWERS *and* LITTLE BOO
(*howling hysterically*)

The queen-mama!
Countenance of silly sheep!
Brush of rusty fire!

152

Silly queen-mama!
Rusty fire on the head!
Stupid an' silly!

(They converge on BATH-SHEBA. ITTAI *draws a long shepherd's knife, leaps between* BATH-SHEBA *and the group—which tumbles backwards.* BATH-SHEBA *exits.* ITTAI *backs and exits. Laughing,* JEROBOAM *drops to the divan. Moments and his laughter subsides almost abruptly. His mood is taken on quickly by all but* TIKVAH, *who continues to laugh. He is silenced by* FOLLOWERS—*collapses behind the divan.)*

JEROBOAM
(Mumbling)
No sanctuary to the north. (LITTLE BOO *crawls close to him*) Go away! Go! Leave! Put her out! (LITTLE BOO *is urged from the stage, whining.* JEROBOAM *broods. He has been shocked into a degree of soberness*) . . . If anything should go wrong—

FOLLOWER 1
(Uneasily)
. . . Wrong?

FOLLOWER 2
. . . But—but nothing can go wrong.

153

MOTHER OF THAT WISDOM

JEROBOAM

(Mostly to himself)

The north would be a trap. He would hunt me out—
Solomon. . . . *She* would. . . . The south! A day's journey
to the south, to Hebron! If all goes well I can return
quickly. If not—Egypt! (*He jumps up. He still staggers*)
Come, we will go! (*He strikes gong, shouts*) Kaza!

FOLLOWER 3

Now? South?

JEROBOAM

At once! (*Servant enters L*) Kaza, the chariots, see
to them! We leave immediately! Speed! (*He strikes gong
as servant exits.*) We will take only gold! Gold and
weapons! And food, yes! (*To another servant who enters
as he slides back small wall panel, pulls out a bag of
gold*) Food for a journey! And weapons for all!—and
torches! Go! (*To* FOLLOWERS) We will leave through
the cellars! Come! (*He starts to exit.*)

FOLLOWER 1

But my lord!—

JEROBOAM

Come, Baal damn you, come!

FOLLOWER 2

My lord!—

MOTHER OF THAT WISDOM

JEROBOAM

Then stay! And die when I next see you! (*He exits.*
The FOLLOWERS *stand.*)

TIKVAH

(He half rises behind divan)

Gran' Prefec'. (*He collapses.*)

Curtain

ACT TWO

Scene III

THE SCENE *An hour later in the hut of a charcoal burner outside the city wall. The hut is dimly lighted, bare of all but necessities. A single wall hole U serves for a window. It is partially covered by a piece of dirty cloth. Through this comes the fitful light of the burner's fire. The single door is U and R. Baskets of charcoal stand against wall L.*

AT RISE *The charcoal burner, an OLD MAN OF GAD, sits in corner R mending baskets. Three city workers, GALILEANS, restlessly prowl the hut: a MAN OF NAPHTALI, a MAN OF ISSACHAR and a MAN OF ZEBULON.*

NAPHTALITE
(He picks up a piece of charcoal)
See. The ways of the men of Judah. Singed wood and he calls it charcoal. *(He hurls the charcoal at the old man)* In Naphtali, old black hands, we would make you eat it!

OLD GADITE
Does a man of Gad char wood to the core for the godless fires of Judah?

156

NAPHTALITE

A Gadite? Forgive me old papa. I would sell them black stones.

OLD GADITE

The men of Naphtali were ever hasty.

ZEBULONITE

Must we wait all night? And where are the two from the aqueduct?

ISSACHARITE

And the Shilonite! Is this the holy man's home, old papa, does he live here?

OLD GADITE

The prophet is here when he comes here.

(*The door opens swiftly. A* MAN OF ASHER *slips in, closes the door, indicates that he is being followed. Excepting the* OLD GADITE, *all hug the wall on both sides of the door, each with a drawn knife. Door opens and a* MAN OF SIMEON, *face covered by his cloak, enters uncertainly. All leap on him.*)

SIMEONITE

Hold, it is *I!* (*He is recognized, released*) Idiots! Must I sing my name like a lost goat?

ASHERITE

Who is the idiot? You dog my heels like a Palace-Guard spy!

157

SIMEONITE

Dog your heels? (*Controlling his irritation, turning away*) You were to be fifty reeds behind me.

NAPHTALITE

You are both idiots. You could have come together.

ASHERITE

Ah, the Naphtalite speaks! I bow to his wisdom. The men of Naphtali are wise beyond all others in the art of night prowling.

NAPHTALITE

Mind your tongue!

ASHERITE

My flock, you mean—if I were in Asher and *had* the flock that was stolen by the raiding men of Naphtali!

NAPHTALITE

Liar! (*Hand to knife.*)

ZEBULONITE

An Asherite cries, "Thief"? (*He laughs.*)

ISSACHARITE

Yes, and an Issacharite! Flocks? Ha! Cattle, crops, even the dogs are not safe near the Zebulon border!

ZEBULONITE

Liar! (*He draws his knife.*)

158

NAPHTALITE

I say it too! Liar! (*Knife out.*)

ASHERITE

Thieves! (*Knife out.*)

ISSACHARITE

Robbers! (*Knife out.*)

SIMEONITE

(*Avoiding the quarrel as the four crouch to maneuver*)
Oh, impressive! Fighting cocks in brainless combat.

(*The door opens and* AHIJAH *enters.*)

AHIJAH

Fools! What unholy folly is this?
(*All five drop to their knees before him.*)

ALL

Rabbi!
Holy man!
Man of God!
Rabbi!
O prophet of God!

AHIJAH

You ask Jehovah's blessing with fratricidal weapons
in your hands? (*The four sheath their knives*) Fools.
Jehovah bless you. Rise. (*All rise*) There will be flesh
enough for your knives among the Judean godless. Sit.

. . . (*The men sit on the floor.*) You will give your lives for Jehovah and His glory in Israel?

ALL

Yes, Yes! Our lives!
Our lives for theirs!
Ten for one!
For God and Israel!
Yes! Gladly! (*They have risen.*)

AHIJAH

Sit, sit. . . . (*The men obey*) The wicked man who calls himself king has overreached himself. He is in our hands. Tomorrow he will proclaim new taxes— (*The men react*) Wait! More men, thousands, are to be dragged out of Israel to slave with you on the foolish aqueduct, on that hope of Satan they call the temple, and on a stinking house of sin dedicated to the gods of the Egyptian harlot! Wait! *Wait!* . . . You men of Galilee— out of Asher, Naphtali, Issachar and Zebulon! Woe to the hand that has struck you! Tomorrow, in payment of the *Judean* debt, all Galilee will be ceded to the king of Tyre!

ASHERITE, NAPHTALITE, ISSACHARITE *and* ZEBULONITE

No! No! Never!
Woe to the hand, the cursed hand!
Death to the tyrant!
Yes, death! Death to his house and seed!

AHIJAH

Peace! *Peace! Peace, I say!* . . . (*The men quiet.*)

160

Save your rage for the morrow. . . . As leaders of your tribes, and men of other tribes, I say this to you. All men must know of this brewing evil! All must know that the hour has come! All must know that tomorrow we *strike!* . . . *(The men react)* At noon a multitude that holds every worker in Jerusalem must gather before the palace. There they must scream their grief, howl their anger! There they must await the signal! There, given the signal, they must rise and destroy the city!

THE GALILEANS

Yes! Destroy it!
Utterly! Utterly!
Till no stone stands!
Tll only blood and ashes remain! We swear it!

SIMEONITE

(Always the contained one)
The signal. What is the signal?

AHIJAH

You will provide the signal. As emissaries of the people you will demand audience with the king. Your demand will be granted. I, Ahijah, tell you so. Face to face with him you will present an ultimatum: With *you* he must appear on the Place of Judgment! There, publicly, he must declare it wicked that Israel be burdened with new taxes! Wicked that more men be taken for labor in Judah! Wicked that temples to false gods be built! And wicked, wicked, *wicked* that Galilee be torn from Israel! . . . *(The men react)* His refusal will be the signal.

161

SIMEONITE

But the host? Can the multitude prevail against the host?

THE GALILEANS
(They turn on him)
See! Because he is not of Galilee!
A turd for the host, you cowardly dog!
You see Galilee betrayed, you pig of the southland!
Pig and *son* of a pig!

SIMEONITE
(Asking for silence with a waved hand)
. . . No, I, too, am angrily concerned regarding Galilee. But *my* revolt is against *all* the evils of the evil king. I *want* his death! Therefore I fear the host.

AHIJAH

Yes. Properly spoken. But be content: There will *be* no host. Benaiah is with us. Azariah is with us.

ASHERITE

. . . A miracle!

ISSACHARITE

Surely only God Himself could make it so!

AHIJAH

Only God—Who is with us. Go now. Seek me tomorrow in the multitude. (*The men kneel before* AHIJAH) Swear to quarrel no more among yourselves.

ALL

We swear.
In Jehovah's name, we swear.
We swear it.
Never. We swear it.
Never.

AHIJAH

Jehovah be with you to make you strong! Jehovah take you into his bosom! Amen! . . . Go. (*The five rise and exit. Pressing his face into his raised hands* AHIJAH *stands motionless.*)

OLD GADITE

Rabbi, can I give you food?

AHIJAH

Food. . . . I have fasted for—days.

OLD GADITE

You must keep up your strength. (*He moves to food box.*)

AHIJAH

Yes. I must be strong.
A little cheese and bread—

OLD GADITE

A little cheese and bread—
(*The door opens.* ITTAI *looks in, steps back.* BATH-SHEBA *enters, her face covered. She drops the cov-*

(ering. AHIJAH *stiffens, turns away, something of* annoyance *in his attitude.)*

BATH-SHEBA
(She moves to him, C. Her voice is low but penetrating. Her questions accuse, express an angry and bitter condemnation)
. . . Why does the prophet Ahijah foul his name by conspiring with treasonous men, with a heathen harlot? . . . (AHIJAH'S *fingers tap his thigh.)* What mockery of prophecy is it that sees the crown of Israel on the head of a godless ingrate? . . . (AHIJAH'S *reaction definitely is annoyance.)* Why does the prophet Ahijah seek to destroy Israel?

AHIJAH
(He gestures in fusty and pettish impatience)
Truly, a woman is Jehovah's little joke!—

BATH-SHEBA
(Her eyes widen)
. . . Joke?

AHIJAH
—may He give me patience—

BATH-SHEBA
(Inspirationally she has seen possibilities of profit in a "Performance." She attacks—loudly—and in operatic indignation)
Woman? Jehovah's little joke?

164

MOTHER OF THAT WISDOM

AHIJAH

Come now, *silence!* I will not—

BATH-SHEBA

Silence unto *you!*—that you speak *sacrilege!*

AHIJAH

Sacrilege? I?

BATH-SHEBA

Foul sacrilege!—may the Great One cleanse your *mouth* and *mind* of it!—with *fire! You,* named as *Holy Man,* by men of *innocence!*

AHIJAH

This is *ridiculous!*—

BATH-SHEBA

Ridiculous *sacrilege, yes!*—rising tainted out of shameful *ignorance! Yours!*

AHIJAH

Ignorance? I have *ignorance?*

BATH-SHEBA

Unholy ignorance!—in that *you,* a *prophet,* know not even the *past!*—know not that Jehovah's *only* joke is in the *ground* of *Hades,* the dead and rotten body and seed of giggling *Lucifer,* hell buried!

AHIJAH

Nonsense! This I knew as a *child!*

165

MOTHER OF THAT WISDOM

BATH-SHEBA
You *knew* this?

AHIJAH
In my mother's *womb* I knew it!

BATH-SHEBA
Yet you know not that *man* is of *woman?*— *Crescendo*) *God's* woman?— (*Fortissimo*) *never, NEVER* of a little *joke* of *JEHOVAH'S?*

AHIJAH
(Recoiling)
Will you *not* burst the *bladders* of my *ears?* . . . You misheard! I used the name of *woman* as a—a *word!*

BATH-SHEBA
Did you, now?

AHIJAH
I *did!* A *sound!* The fancy of the mindless tongue flicked a jot of breath to—to voice a mindless mood!

BATH-SHEBA
By Jehovah! Your answer is like nothing but a windy *bowel-verse,* breathed without *sense* from a camel's *rump!*

AHIJAH
Silence! You grow too bold! I made truthful answer to silly word and greater fool!—*yours* and *you!*—as, by the will of God, I must *always* do!

MOTHER OF THAT WISDOM

BATH-SHEBA

Always?

AHIJAH

Always!

BATH-SHEBA

Make truthful answer, then, to what you *did* not answer! *This*: You conspire with *vile men* and a *heathen harlot! Why?* (*Fortissimo, closer*) You seek to *crown* a *godless ingrate! Why?* (*Molto fortissimo, in his face*) *You would destroy Israel! WHY!* (*Momentarily* AHIJAH *is overpowered. He wilts.*)

AHIJAH
(Wearily)

. . . The tool that carves the name of God on the hearts of men may be foul or fair. God is pleased if it carves well.

BATH-SHEBA
(She is honestly appalled)
. . . And *Israel?*

AHIJAH

I lead Israel to God.

BATH-SHEBA
(Her "performance" is over)
You lead Israel to agony.

MOTHER OF THAT WISDOM

AHIJAH

(Rekindling)

To agony, yes! To *appointed* agony!

BATH-SHEBA

To *what?*

AHIJAH

Down the road of sorrow! Into the valleys of woe, where tears and suffering shall be their drink and meat! —until the coming of the Messiah.

BATH-SHEBA

That is madness! Ancient madness! The Messiah will come to a strong and worthy people, not to a race mad-bent on its own destruction! From the very lips of the prophet Nathan I know this to be true!

AHIJAH

Nathan! (*He is swept by hatred*) Nathan spoke with a corrupted tongue from out of the soft bosom of David! Had he been cast forth by his king as something unclean he would have spoken as I speak! With a tongue as hard and bitter as the bread I eat and the stones that are my bed!— (*He knows he has betrayed himself.*)

BATH-SHEBA

. . . Then it is that:—a personal grievance. You fight my son because he rejected you.

AHIJAH

To reject God's prophet is to reject God!

168

MOTHER OF THAT WISDOM

BATH-SHEBA
(She feels grief)

Oh, Ahijah—hate Solomon if you must! But the people—the road of sorrow—tears, suffering— The Jews have had so much of suffering! The end of endless suffering is death! Is that what you want? Death for the Jews? . . . (*Faced stonily away* AHIJAH *makes no response.* BATH-SHEBA *crosses slowly to the door—pauses*) I believe Jehovah loves Israel. I do not *believe* He wants His loved ones to suffer. If I did I could not believe in Jehovah.

AHIJAH

You are a woman, therefore a fool.

BATH-SHEBA

Perhaps. Most of my life I have worked hard to give that impression. . . . May you find peace, Ahijah.

(She exits. ITTAI, *reaching in, pulls shut the door.)*

AHIJAH
(Eyes burning, body rigid, he raises
vibrating hands to heaven)

Almighty Father! . . . (*The* OLD GADITE *hugs the floor.*)

Almighty Father! This is Thy will! A sign! Give me a sign!

(AHIJAH *stiffens spasmodically. Choking in a convulsive seizure he falls. . . . He lies as dead for mo-*

169

ments—stirs. The OLD GADITE *bathes his head with a wet cloth. . . . He rises.)*

OLD GADITE
Holy Man, let me give you food.

AHIJAH
(He is exalted)
Who breaks bread with Jehovah needs no earthly food! (*He exits.*)

Curtain

ACT TWO

Scene IV

The Scene   *Again the chamber in* BATH-SHEBA's *pavilion, an hour later.*

At Rise   BATH-SHEBA *is discovered seated behind a small table L of C.* KINYRAS, *the Wise Man of Tyre, sits beside her.* ABISHAG *sits R, working with her needle.* ITTAI, *near her, squats on the floor, repairing his lute, the better to gaze at her. Old* MAACAH *is in her chair U and R.*

Several bags of drugs and spices lie on the top of one of the treasure baskets. A similar bag, opened, lies on the table before BATH-SHEBA.

KINYRAS
(Fingering the contents of the bag, a gray powder)

The men of Ophir keep their secrets well. "The powder brings sleep," they said. "We will sell it to you. The secret of its composition is ours." But it fulfills their boast. I used it on the ships to bring sleep in sickness.

BATH-SHEBA

"The contents of a rocknut shell." It seems a small quantity.

171

KINYRAS

Its strength is remarkable. That amount will entrance
for some eight hours. More would be dangerous.

BATH-SHEBA

Then to bring sleep to—one hundred men?

KINYRAS

One hundred? (BATH-SHEBA *gazes at him blandly.*)
(*He gestures.*) One hundred times the quantity. But
here: I have a device. Fever takes me in certain damp-
ness and I use a powdered bark. This dispenses it.
(KINYRAS *lifts free the small blue and jeweled casket that
dangles from his neck, as described in Act One.*)

BATH-SHEBA

How beautiful!

KINYRAS

Press down this release, you see, and it drops just the
contents of the rocknut shell. Accept it with my deathless
regard.

BATH-SHEBA

My dear friend. I will keep it always.

KINYRAS

May it serve you.

BATH-SHEBA

And now I have a further favor to ask of you.

MOTHER OF THAT WISDOM

KINYRAS

Ask it.

BATH-SHEBA

Well, we have a scandal in the harem. Three of the concubines are with child—and not by Solomon.

KINYRAS

The work of Hebrew angels, undoubtedly.

BATH-SHEBA

Of rascally guards. The punishment is stoning, of course; but they are nice girls—young and pretty—so I thought if—?

KINYRAS

. . . My caravan leaves tomorrow evening.

BATH-SHEBA

Ah, Kinyras, you have the heart of a Jew!

KINYRAS
(He laughs)
Naturally. Your late husband was the first to say that Semites *all* are brother people.

BATH-SHEBA

Yes, we are—and should *not* be divided. That was David's dream, you know—to unite the Semites.

KINYRAS

David's dreams. They were proper dreams.

BATH-SHEBA

You *were* his friend; I know.

KINYRAS

More. I led King Hiram's first mission of friendship
to Israel. David called me brother, and kissed me. He
talked. . . . Of all men, I believe he was the greatest man.

BATH-SHEBA

Oh, he was, wasn't he? Oh, he was! . . . (*Dabbing at
her eyes*) And he was so sweet, too.

KINYRAS
(*He chuckles*)

The captain Joab once said to me: "What a god he
would make if he were not so damned pleasant."

BATH-SHEBA
(*Somberly*)

. . . Yes—Joab.

MAACAH
(*She has stirred sharply in her
chair at the name of Joab*)

Joab! Yes! It was *he!* He thrust the darts! He slew
my son! He slew my Absalom!

BATH-SHEBA

Maacah! (*To* ABISHAG, *as she rises, crosses quickly
U*) Wine!

174

MAACAH

Dead, dead, dead! My son is dead!

BATH-SHEBA

No, no, Maacah!

MAACAH

(She staggers to her feet)

The guilty hands! The bloody hands! Jehovah's curse
on the bloody hands! (*She collapses to the floor.*)

BATH-SHEBA

(Puts a cup to MAACAH's *lips.)*

Drink, Maacah. Drink. (*And to* ITTAI:) The gong.
(ITTAI *strikes the gong.*) There. Be comforted. All is
well. (*To* ITTAI *and* ABISHAG) Help me to lift her.

MAACAH

(To ITTAI*)*

. . . Absalom? Is there news?

BATH-SHEBA

Soon, Maacah, soon. (BATH-SHEBA, *with* ITTAI *and*
ABISHAG, *lifts her into her chair.*)

MAACAH

Soon. Yes. Please, God, soon.

*(Servants have entered. They lift her chair, carry
her out,* ABISHAG *at her side,* ITTAI *following.)*

KINYRAS

The gods do very ill to take the soul and leave the body. (*He sees that* BATH-SHEBA *is staring down at her hands. He turns away.*)

BATH-SHEBA

(*Remorse choking her she goes to her knees*)
Forgive. . . . Forgive. . . .

KINYRAS

(*He moves to her, touches her head*)
It is said in Tyre that only the great can sin greatly.

BATH-SHEBA

(*Moments and she gives him her hand, rises, sits*)
. . . You see—it was *I* who—

KINYRAS

Hush, child.

BATH-SHEBA

. . . Can there be forgiveness, Kinyras—for great sin?

KINYRAS

Our gods, yours and mine, are not kin. But there can be peace—through service. This, surely.

BATH-SHEBA

Peace would be forgiveness. . . . Yes. . . . (*With abrupt effort she alters her mood as* ABISHAG *and* ITTAI *enter*) Well! Thank you, dears. And now just one more favor, Kinyras?

176

KINYRAS

A thousand.

BATH-SHEBA
*(She thanks him with her eyes in a
fleeting return of her former mood)*
. . . Come here, children. . . . (ABISHAG *and* ITTAI
obey.) You know about this Abishag child, Kinyras?

KINYRAS

David's little Shunamite.

BATH-SHEBA

And now Solomon's—and a maid still in spite of both
of them.

KINYRAS

Tch, tch, tch!

BATH-SHEBA

And you have seen Ittai, the king's poet and musician?

KINYRAS

I have.

BATH-SHEBA

Kinyras, they are rapidly dying of love for each other.

KINYRAS

Dear me! What a pity they could not join my caravan.

177

MOTHER OF THAT WISDOM

BATH-SHEBA

Oh, it is! They could live in Tyre in great happiness.

KINYRAS

Truly a pity.

ABISHAG

(She drops to her knees)

My lady! Say it is true, say it is true!

BATH-SHEBA

Of course it is true!

ITTAI

(On his knees)

Oh, my lady, Jehovah bless you!

BATH-SHEBA

And you, my dear ones. And in time, when I have smoothed the royal hackles, you can return—if you so choose.

ITTAI

(To KINYRAS*)*

Our eternal gratitude, my lord!

ABISHAG

Jehovah bless you, my lord!

KINYRAS

May all the gods bless you, my children. We leave from the north gate tomorrow at sundown. Rise now. *(To* BATH-SHEBA*)* I shall go, my lady.

178

MOTHER OF THAT WISDOM

BATH-SHEBA
(Rising)
Farewell, Kinyras! . . . May we meet again.

KINYRAS
I am sure we will—somewhere. All blessings! (*He exits L.*)

BATH-SHEBA
(Eyes holding, after his exit)
And for you. (*She turns to see* ITTAI *and* ABISHAG *embracing*) Just a little longer, children.

SERVANT
(He enters L, goes to knee)
The lord Benaiah has come and has been waiting, my lady.

BATH-SHEBA
Hold till I send. (*To* ITTAI, *as* SERVANT *exits*) Bring in the captain Azariah, Ittai. (ITTAI *exits R.*)
(BATH-SHEBA *goes to her knees in prayer.* ABISHAG *imitates her. . . .* ITTAI *enters R with* AZARIAH. ITTAI *goes to his knees. A moment and* AZARIAH *kneels. . . .* BATH-SHEBA *rises. The others rise.* BATH-SHEBA *to* ITTAI)
Send in the lord Benaiah. Then go to bed. (ITTAI *exits L.*)

AZARIAH
(He is terrified)
My lady!

179

BATH-SHEBA

I have given you my word: you will not be harmed.
(*To* ABISHAG) Go to bed, Abishag. (*And, as* ABISHAG
exits L) Alone, dear. (*To* AZARIAH) Behave manfully—
remembering that *now* you are *right*. (AZARIAH *straightens.*)

(BENAIAH *enters L. At sight of the now rigid* AZA-
RIAH, *he halts. He draws his sword slowly and starts for*
AZARIAH) Sheath your sword, Benaiah. (BENAIAH
pauses) *Sheath your sword!*

BENAIAH
(He obeys)
Then remove the dog from my sight!

BATH-SHEBA
(To AZARIAH)
Go. (*Gesturing toward room R from which he came.*
AZARIAH *exits, head up*) He was not false to you, Ben-
aiah. I tricked him.

BENAIAH
Then he is fatally stupid, which is equally bad.

BATH-SHEBA
He is young. As he grows older he will gain wisdom.
Finally, perhaps, he will become wise enough to have
original ideas regarding treason.

BENAIAH
I know your opinion of what I do, my lady. It has no

weight. The thing is done. Save your breath and go to bed. (*Turning to make for the doors L.*)

BATH-SHEBA

The thing is *not* done! And if it were I would want neither breath *nor* bed and *those doors are barred!* (BEN-AIAH *draws his sword to hack the doors*) By Jehovah, Benaiah, must you behave like a dolt?

BENAIAH

Have those doors opened!

BATH-SHEBA

When it suits my fancy! Do you actually think that I shall sit here like a dull pleasure-wench and do nothing?

BENAIAH

Now who is the dolt? There is nothing you *can* do!

BATH-SHEBA
(*A shade* too *much hauteur*)

In view of the years you have known me, and all you know *about* me, to say such a thing is downright insulting!

BENAIAH

Insulting? . . . Now, look here, do not try to work your zany stunt on *me!*

BATH-SHEBA

Stunt?

181

BENAIAH

I know you are no nitwit! And I repeat, there is nothing you *can* do! I am the army, Ahijah is the people, and the Nile baggage is Solomon's mind!

BATH-SHEBA

Benaiah, must we quarrel personally?

BENAIAH

Who is quarreling? I am merely—(*He stops, eyes her steadily.*)

BATH-SHEBA

(*She drops her head and drops pretense*)

All right, Benaiah—I will be good—if you will tell me why you are doing this thing.

BENAIAH

For Israel.

BATH-SHEBA

Jeroboam will make a better king than the son of David?

BENAIAH

He can be handled.

BATH-SHEBA

You want a king you can handle.

BENAIAH

Do not trick me with words! A weak ruler is bad

182

enough. When he is stubborn in the bargain— (*He gestures*) A little more of Solomon's dove-begotten fancy for peace and there would *be* no Israel—as a nation.

BATH-SHEBA
(Sharply)
You think his desire for peace is rooted in weakness?

BENAIAH
In watery salt paste!

BATH-SHEBA
Vah! The one thing in which he is completely strong! (BENAIAH *gestures*) Yes! For years you have urged him to make war! You have met rigid resistance!

BENAIAH
I granted his stubbornness.

BATH-SHEBA
No! You have closed yourself to his logic! to his *studied* belief in peaceful expansion! Weakness! It is in this that he is most like David!

BENAIAH
Do not talk like a woman! David was a warrior. And if he could see the military mess his son has made of the host he would vomit!

BATH-SHEBA
That is unfair, un*true*, Benaiah! Solomon has a host such as David never had!

BENAIAH

Pah! Fifty thousand bored men playing at soldiers!

BATH-SHEBA

Then you want war solely to make killers of bored men.

BENAIAH

I want an aggressive, conquering army that will build Israel!

BATH-SHEBA

No, bloat Israel! Till she bursts of her own corrupt weight and dies! As Egypt is dying!

BENAIAH

Egypt is dying *because* her army has gone to pot! And there is my point. A free hand for two years and I will smash Egypt into groveling ruin!

BATH-SHEBA

And you will begin by destroying Jerusalem. (BEN-AIAH *gestures*) Oh, yes! I know Ahijah's plans!

BENAIAH

All right, a city dies. But a nation lives, an empire is born.

BATH-SHEBA

That is just something you read somewhere and you know it.

BENAIAH

I *never* read! And by the Almighty I shall not stand here and listen to any more drivel! (BENAIAH strides toward doors, pulling sword.)

BATH-SHEBA

No! *No!* (*She droops, sincerely weeping—as* BENAIAH *yanks at doors—as they open—to* BENAIAH's *momentary confusion. He regards doors . . . looks over at the weeping woman—whom he has known in warm friendship and, unknown to her, in more than warm affection for many years. . . . He sheaths his sword, closes doors, crosses to her. . . .*)

BENAIAH

(*His hand moves to touch her. He draws it back*)
. . . My lady. . . . Solomon's life will not be taken. Nor yours.

BATH-SHEBA

(*She shakes her head. Moments, and she
partially controls her tears*)
. . . Benaiah—the temple.

BENAIAH

. . . My lady. (*Touched with self-consciousness*) In matters of religion I am—I do not find myself in spiritual accord with—my lady! (*Incongruously carried away*) In a matter of regard, *personal* regard, I would like you to know at last that the giving of my blood and life for *you, Bath-sheba*, would be a gesture that I would

—that is— (*Recovering, as* BATH-SHEBA *turns to stare at him*) for your *content!*—uh, *welfare!* Yes! But it is *not,* you see! Not at all! Quite not!

BATH-SHEBA

Benaiah, what *are* you trying to say?

BENAIAH

Just that, my lady! The temple! I am not a religious man!

BATH-SHEBA

(Understanding comes through to her—but there is no time for that. She shakes her head)

. . . The temple is *more* than religion, Benaiah. It was David's dream of a symbol; of Jehovah's inevitable dominance, of the high destiny of the Jew. Oh, Benaiah, allow it to be built! Once it is built it will never die! Once it is built it can be *torn down* and it will still live! I know not *how* I know that but I do! . . . And how can I face David if it is not built? He trusted me. (*She weeps*) He will scold me.

BENAIAH

(Head lowered)

. . . And he trusted me—in a larger sense.

BATH-SHEBA

Not larger! Oh, my dear, can you not believe that *I* know what he would have wanted? Benaiah, I was his darling; through the night hours, when he spoke of what was deep in his heart. And I swear to you that what was deepest was a great weariness of killing, a yearning for peace, for things that come *out* of peace. Benaiah, he had a vision! He saw the people gathered around a splendid fountain that played before the temple steps. And they sang and danced in happy praise of God! And not one belly was empty, and not one heart held fear! And temple, fountain, security, abundance: peace would bring them. A warrior! Yes, he fought! Because he was a brave man and the times were such that only war could bring unity and peace. Because he was *God's* man —for peace *and* war. . . . Benaiah . . . (BENAIAH's *head is still down*) Benaiah! Before God can you deny that your treason has only one object?—to perpetuate your name as Israel's greatest warrior?

BENAIAH
(He sighs)

Very well. Not as the greatest. David was that. But Saul!— (*Kindling*) a great king, a patriot; and until he found David, a military amateur given to sporadic raids! And Joab—the great Joab, fabulous hero, genius of war! Pah! He was an excellent captain of thousands who could follow a battle plan!—David's! And I? Let me die tonight and what will be written? "Benaiah: an obscure captain who slew the mighty Joab!"—

BATH-SHEBA

Benaiah—

BENAIAH

Oh, yes!—no more than that! Treason. Treason
to what? To the flabby ideals of a weak prince? I am a
creature of war, all of me, by Jehovah's will! I am a
sword, no good for anything *but* war! And for five years
I have been forced to sit and corrode in this bog of
peace! Well, that is over. I am going to do my work so
that what is written will not shame my ghost! If it serves
Israel, so much the better. And it *will* serve Israel. Because most surely I shall destroy the reptile Jeroboam!
—and that slimy Edomite pretender!—and all *Egyptians*
that come against me! . . . But enough. I go. . . .

(BATH-SHEBA *stands with lowered head*) I am sorry,
my lady. More than you know. Farewell. (*He crosses—
opens doors.*)

BATH-SHEBA

*(Her head coming up in sudden awareness of something
significant in his penultimate words)*

No, no! Wait! You said—*Wait, I implore* you!
(BENAIAH *waits.*)

(*She moves, murmuring her thoughts*) . . . Egypt—
Edom. . . . War. . . . (*Then abruptly*) Well, heaven
mark me as a lack-brain! You shall *have* your war! Shut
the doors!

BENAIAH

My lady! The time for trickery is—

BATH-SHEBA

Do not talk nonsense, it is inevitable, your war! Shut

188

the *doors!* . . . (BENAIAH *obeys*) Listen to me! At this moment the Egyptian trollop is well on her way to Egypt, is she not?

BENAIAH
If she got rid of Solomon.

BATH-SHEBA
And that Edomite pretender—Ad'hotep, or whatever—by now he is nearing Edom, is he not?

BENAIAH
Or Egypt—probably.

BATH-SHEBA
Well? Must I engrave it? Your own plan gives Egypt and Edom an open road to Judah!

BENAIAH
Not mine—Jeroboam's.

BATH-SHEBA
But the *fact!* They will strike immediately! It is war!

BENAIAH
(He is impressed)
. . . But Solomon.

BATH-SHEBA
Did Solomon build a host to have it sit on its bottom while Israel is invaded?

189

MOTHER OF THAT WISDOM

BENAIAH

I wonder.

BATH-SHEBA

Cheap cynicism! This was the very purpose of his host! Defensive war!

BENAIAH

Ah, there it is: defensive.

BATH-SHEBA

A *term!* Did David always defend by attacking, or did he not? And very well you know that with the pharaoh's pompous rabble on the run you will chase them to the Nile!

BENAIAH

By Abraham! Perhaps you have something!

BATH-SHEBA

Yes. War.

BENAIAH

If I could be sure of Solomon.

BATH-SHEBA

Benaiah: The trollop is gone. If you can be sure of me, you can be sure of Solomon.

BENAIAH

(He regards her, decides)

. . . Right! Now, let me see: The *Northern* Host, I

190

must bring it down. Damnation, it will take days, and we *must* strike first! I must go, my lady. I shall start north for Megiddo immediately.

BATH-SHEBA

Then you *will* stand by Solomon.

BENAIAH

Eh? Of course!—

BATH-SHEBA
(Murmuring tearfully)
Praise Jehovah!

BENAIAH

—And if he had listened to *me* the *full* host would be in the south right now! But no, the great pharaoh might think we were— Now, come, come—tears! How odd that the best of women can not be manly. Now I *must* go.

BATH-SHEBA

But Benaiah! The revolution!

BENAIAH

Oh, yes, that, Well, we can't stop Ahijah now; we shall have to put it down.

BATH-SHEBA

The soldiers will be turned loose on the people.

191

BENAIAH

Naturally. But Azariah can work gently. He is still here, I had forgotten. Have him in.

BATH-SHEBA

In a moment. . . . Benaiah: Whatever happens tomorrow Solomon must face it himself, without the aid of force. (BENAIAH *looks at her*) You say he is weak. *I* know he *can* be *greatly* strong. He *must* be or he will fall, and Israel with him—when I am gone.

BENAIAH

You do not quell revolution without force.

BATH-SHEBA

You quell the spirit of revolution with justice.

BENAIAH

If you have time. (*He has a thought*) Perhaps you have! Look here, the woman is gone: why not *see* Solomon, try to talk him into reasonable decisions?

BATH-SHEBA

And tell him of the conspiracy? (BENAIAH *feels his beard.*) Short of that nothing could change him in time. No. This might almost have been planned, Benaiah—as a test. I have never loved him weakly. And surely the quality of love is contagious. So I *must* believe in his potential strength—and let him meet the test.

BENAIAH

Test. Perhaps I am stupid. Without the City Host to hold it the mob will hit this palace like an angry sea.

BATH-SHEBA

The palace guard could hold for a time, could it not?

BENAIAH

For minutes.

BATH-SHEBA

That is enough.

BENAIAH
(He gestures)

Very well, what do I do? Order the troops to play dead? If they disobey the king's orders he will have my life.

BATH-SHEBA

You go north at once. *Now* you instruct Azariah to follow my orders. If the king is disobeyed he will never know it. I give you my word.

BENAIAH
(He studies her—capitulates)

I am a mouse, just a mouse. *(He crosses R, calls off)* Azariah! *(To* BATH-SHEBA*)* Don't mislead the young simpleton disastrously, I am fond of him. (AZARIAH *enters, goes to his knee)* Get up. (AZARIAH *rises.* BENAIAH *regards him)* It is very becoming, that ring in your nose.

193

How do you like mine? (AZARIAH's *hand starts to his nose, drops*) The queen-mother has orders for you. Obey them. (Crossing to doors L) Good-night, my lady! (*He pauses at doors, looks at her*) ... Fortune with you.

BATH-SHEBA

Thank you, Benaiah. Good-night! . . . (BENAIAH *exits.*)

Well! Sit down, Azariah—here. (AZARIAH *sits by the table.* BATH-SHEBA *sits, regards him benignly*) I have a plan. The captains of your City Host: they take the noon meal together?

AZARIAH

Yes, my lady.

BATH-SHEBA

You number how many captains?

AZARIAH

Some two hundred, my lady.

BATH-SHEBA

Who would give orders to the soldiers if the captains were all drunk?

AZARIAH

Drunk, my lady?

BATH-SHEBA

Quite drunk?

194

MOTHER OF THAT WISDOM

AZARIAH

I would, my lady.

BATH-SHEBA

And if you were drunk?

AZARIAH

I never get drunk, my lady!

BATH-SHEBA

You are going to, Azariah. I have here a little device. (*She takes up* KINYRAS'*s jeweled casket. A curtain starts slowly down.*) It holds a powder. When the powder is dropped into wine, all who drink the wine will sleep as the dead for eight hours—

Curtain

ACT TWO

Scene V

THE SCENE   *The Porch of Judgment, as in Act One, Scene I, the following day at noon.*

AT RISE   *A few palace officials and servants are discovered arranging stools and low tables for transaction of business. Also discovered are the five guards—*HETH, MEMUCAN, BICHRI, ISHUI *and* HOSAH—*of Act One, Scene I in their familiar places.*

The group of four young idlers is revealed, the same four as in Act One, Scene I. They stand at the top of stairway U observing an assembling offstage multitude as they languidly sniff at their perfume sticks.

The upstage curtains are open, the low noise of the multitude coming in.

IDLER A
Sullen-seeming brutes, eh?

IDLER B
Not exactly happy-sounding.

IDLER C
I was in the market district this morning when the proclamation was made. I went away quickly.

IDLER D

I wonder what they will do when they hear about Galilee?

IDLER C

Baal, yes! But is it decided?

IDLER D

So it is said 'neath the whisper tree.
                (The crowd noise swells.)

IDLER B

Perhaps we should go home and lock up.

IDLER A

We should, you know. We frighten so easily.

(The four laugh. ZABUD, *the grand Prefect, enters L. Behind him come Elihoreph and Ahiah, the Scribes, bearing clay tablets and the tools of their trade. Jehoshaphat, the Recorder, follows them.*

All on stage, excepting guards, bend a knee to ZABUD.*)*

ZABUD

Jehovah with us, my friends! *(The crowd noise swells.)* Well! They have their lungs with them today!

IDLER A

Very terrifying, my lord. Has the Galilean question been decided, my lord?

ZABUD

By whom?

IDLER A

By the king.

ZABUD

But I am not the king. (*To Scribe*) Elihoreph, the grain-tax record.

(IDLER A *wrinkles his nose and sniffs his stick.* BATH-SHEBA *enters L. She pauses, held by the crescendo-ing roar of the multitude. All but the guards go to one knee.*)

BATH-SHEBA

Oh, rise, rise! (ABISHAG *enters.* BATH-SHEBA *starts for the steps UC. A thrown rock strikes a pillar and falls into the pavilion.*) Close the curtains! (*A guard obeys. The noise is muffled.* BATH-SHEBA *mounts the steps, peers between the curtains.*)

ZABUD

Careful, my lady.

BATH-SHEBA

The steps are thinly guarded. (*To the guard* BICHRI) Where is the captain of the palace guard?

BICHRI

In the armor room, my lady.

BATH-SHEBA

Bring him to me at once. (*To remaining guards, as* BICHRI *exits R.*) The rest of you: join the guards on the steps. (*Guards hesitate as the mob roar swells*) What, timid? Such virile wall climbers? Go! (*Guards exit through curtains.*)

IDLER A

The Israelites seem a bit uneasy, my lady.

BATH-SHEBA

Do we?

IDLER B

He means the workers, my lady.

BATH-SHEBA

Oh? We are a very uneasy race, we Jews. We aspire. Strangers find us restless.

IDLER A

Oh, we are Jews, my lady! But we are Judahites.

BATH-SHEBA

Dear, dear! Try not to be ashamed of it. (*She turns away*) Forgive me, Zabud, I have not greeted you. And Jehoshaphat. It is apparent the tax and labor decisions have been proclaimed.

ZABUD

Yes, my lady.

199

BATH-SHEBA

And Galilee: the king will meet Hiram's demand?

ZABUD

Only in part. (*Quietly*) My lady, I am rather alarmed. You noticed soldiers in the multitude?

BATH-SHEBA

Yes.

ZABUD

They wear the white plume of the Jerusalem Host. It is disturbing. I have sent two couriers to the barracks but they have not returned.

BATH-SHEBA

Then you have done all you can do.

ZABUD

Azariah should *be* here, you know.

ZADOK

(*The Chief Priest enters. He wears full priestly regalia. He is followed by* THREE PRIESTS. *The head of one,* NABOTH, *is bandaged. All, including* BATH-SHEBA, *go to both knees)*
Jehovah's blessing upon you! Jehovah's blessing upon Israel! Jehovah's wisdom and love in the minds and hearts of all who guide Israel! Amen!

MOTHER OF THAT WISDOM

BATH-SHEBA
(Rising)

Zadok, welcome!

ZADOK

My lady! My lord Zabud! (*The mob roar swells.*) My son is not here?

ZABUD

No, my lord. I was just regretting Azariah's absence.

ZADOK

And Benaiah?

BATH-SHEBA

I believe Benaiah was called suddenly to the north. Has this rabbi had an accident? (*Indicating the bandaged* NABOTH.)

ZADOK

This is Naboth, a temple priest. Tell them, rabbi.

NABOTH

They stoned us in our tents, my lady, from the temple works.

ZABUD

The temple workers stoned you?

NABOTH

Some were workers, my lord. But this we do not understand! Some were soldiers of the City Host.

201

ZABUD

U'm. (*To* ZADOK) There are more out there.

ZADOK

It is strange. And the city is full of rumors.

NABOTH

As we came to the palace it was cried that the captains of the host have all been slain.

SECOND PRIEST

Some said that Galilee is to be given to Tyre.

THIRD PRIEST

In the marketplace it was whispered that Solomon has fled to Egypt and Jeroboam will be king.

ZABUD

Jeroboam! (*He laughs.*)

ZADOK

Where *is* Jeroboam?

ZABUD

Yes, where? One would think *I* was Overseer of Labor. I have had to do his work. (ZABUD *indicates tablets*).

BOZ

(*He enters R. He wears the golden armor of a captain.* BICHRI *follows him. Bends a knee to* BATH-SHEBA)
Boz, Captain of the Palace Guard, my lady!

202

BATH-SHEBA

Yes, Boz. How many guards have you in the palace?

BOZ

Four score, my lady, and four captains.

BATH-SHEBA

Assemble them and mass them on the palace steps—
by order of the king.

BOZ

Yes, my lady.

BATH-SHEBA

And Boz: The steps must be held.

(A distant shophar sounds.)

IDLER D

The shophar!

IDLER B
(At the curtains)
It came from the *temple* works!

ZADOK

What sacrilege is this?

IDLER *A*
(Peering between curtains)
By Baal, yes, they are leaving the works. Look at
them pour out!

203

IDLER B

The silly goats, they are all coming here!

BATH-SHEBA

The steps, Boz! You must *hold* them!

BOZ

With the sword, my lady?

BATH-SHEBA

No! No, no! Without! At all *costs* without!

ZADOK

Captain! The movements of the City Host!—what *of* them?

BOZ

I don't know, my lord. I wait word from the captain Azariah.

ZADOK

Can you not *send* for word?

BOZ

Massed people block the streets, my lord.

BATH-SHEBA

Go, now!

(BOZ *exits R,* BICHRI *following. The crowd roar swells.)*

204

IDLER B
(At the curtains)
I say! See the brutes come!

IDLER D
You know, this is getting a bit moldy. (*To* BATH-SHEBA) My lady, do think it advisable that we should go home?

BATH-SHEBA
I think it advisable that you cease to impersonate unopened buds. . . . Zabud, the Galilean grant, let me see it. (ZABUD *hands her the tablet, she studies it.*)

ZADOK
(To the FOUR IDLERS, *who are loftily sniffing at their sniffers)*
Must you sniff at those things? In David's court *men* carried swords, not perfume sticks.

IDLER A
The very words of my father, my lord Rabbi! (*Drawing back his outer robe, revealing a sword.*)

IDLERS B, C *and* D
(The same)
And mine!
And mine!
And *mine!*

ZADOK
(He smiles)
Perhaps they had not thought of sniffers.

MOTHER OF THAT WISDOM

BATH-SHEBA
(Reading)
"The towns of Hazrah, Taadish and Keda, and the lands of these places to the borders of Tyre." They are how close to the borders?

ZABUD
Practically *on* the borders—and populated largely by Phoenicians.

BATH-SHEBA
But then this surely is a small concession.

ZABUD
And a bargain for Israel if King Hiram accepts it. But how will the noisome prophet interpret it to the people?

BATH-SHEBA
That man *is* a boil on the very nose of my son!

AHISHER
(He enters L, strikes his gong)
The king!

(SOLOMON enters with four guards. A small retinue follows, one of whom carries the inlaid wooden container holding the crown. ITTAI is absent. Only ZADOK, by grace of his robes, does not kneel.)

206

SOLOMON

Jehovah's blessing! Rise! (*The mob roar swells. He ascends to curtains, yanks them open. The voice of the multitude rolls over him. He snaps the curtains closed*) What folly is this? Azariah! . . . (*To* ZADOK) Your son, rabbi, where is he?

ZADOK

I do not know, my lord.

ZABUD

He is not in the palace, my lord.

SOLOMON

Then send for him! Or do you enjoy this music?

ZABUD

Two couriers have gone out, my lord. They have not returned.

SOLOMON

Aggravation! Benaiah! Where is Benaiah?

ZABUD

(*He looks at* BATH-SHEBA—*who seems abstracted*) . . . He was called north, my lord.

SOLOMON

With no word to *me!* (*He scans the company*) And Jeroboam: Unavoidably detained by an empty wine cask, perhaps?

MOTHER OF THAT WISDOM

ZABUD

We know only that he is absent, my lord.

SOLOMON

Have him collected then!—by his heels if he is too drunk to walk! (*And as* ZABUD *starts exit*) Not at the moment!—we have business.

GUARD CAPTAIN

(*He steps through parted curtains at stair-head*)
My lord! The West Wing Guard is placed!

SOLOMON

. . . The what?—is what?

BATH-SHEBA

On the steps, my son. The protection is thin. I thought it would be a good idea.

SOLOMON

You thought! By Jehovah, am I the king or a crowned swill pot? (*To* GUARD CAPTAIN) Very well, *go!*

(*As* GUARD CAPTAIN *exits C* SOLOMON *ascends steps quickly to curtains, muttering*) "The West Wing Guard" indeed! (*He parts curtains widely, looks out and down. The voice of the multitude swells in. A single voice is heard above it, shouting:* "Jeroboam! Jeroboam for king!" SOLOMON *snaps the curtains closed, descends steps.*)

"Jeroboam for king." That is a noxious little idea. Smells like the work of my friend Ahijah.

ZADOK

Every mob has its cranks, my lord.

SOLOMON

U'm. But I fancy the lord Jeroboam has left Jerusalem. We must hunt him out. Well, to business! (*He reclines on divan*) The new decrees do not seem to be popular. Do the fools think progress is bought without pain? Let me have the tablets.

BATH-SHEBA

There are degrees of pain, my son. All men scream under agony.

SOLOMON

To the weak all pain is agony. Israel is weak.

BATH-SHEBA

My son—

SOLOMON

Yes! Petulant, immature, given to the whining of the growing child! What would you have me do, sit like a hidebound tribal priest while she slides into economic ruin?

BATH-SHEBA

No, my son.

MOTHER OF THAT WISDOM

SOLOMON

Mind the harem, my mother, and forget the state.
. . . (*He takes up tablets*) The grain tax. This will be
followed by a spiteful decrease in production. Keep the
royal granaries full. A man with hungry children will kiss
the hand that holds food. . . . Oil tax. The same. . . .
Fuel. The same. . . . Linen, leather and wool. Proclaim
the cancellation of this tax.

ZABUD

Cancellation, my lord?

SOLOMON

It will have a good effect. There would be little buy-
ing in any event. . . . The labor levy. There will be trouble here. Let the drafts be sudden and well supported by
force. Oh, and we will need a new labor minister. The
lord Jeroboam can hardly be that *and* king. (*General
restrained laughter.*) Find me one, Zabud.

BOZ

(*With second captain, he parts curtains at stair-
head, enters*)

My lord the king! The East Wing Guard is in position!

SOLOMON

(*Sourly*)

East Wing, West Wing, Will there be more?

BOZ

Yes, my lord. The North Wing will sally from the chariot ramp at my order.

SOLOMON

By my beard, this is—! Very well, very well, *sally them!*—to the music of pipes and strings if the lady *Bathsheba* fancies such! . . . Go!

BOZ
(With exit of second captain)

My lord—if I may ask: Will the City Host be ordered to riot duty?

SOLOMON

Ah—you are advising this?

BOZ

If I may, my lord.

SOLOMON

You may *not!* The City Host is the command of the lord Azariah!—who will move appropriately without advice from underlings! Now, *go!* (BOZ *bends his knee, exits*) . . . Will the *slaves* instruct me next? . . . (*He picks up a tablet*) Galilee. Where is the Tyrian emissary?

AHISHER

He waits, my lord.

MOTHER OF THAT WISDOM

SOLOMON

Have him in. (*To* ZABUD, *as* AHISHER *exits R*) You think well of this?

ZABUD

Quite well, my lord.

SOLOMON

Zadok?

ZADOK

I do, my lord.

SOLOMON
(*To* BATH-SHEBA)
You have seen it, my lady?

BATH-SHEBA

Yes, my lord. I think that the grant, as written, would be much to the benefit of Israel—

SOLOMON

As written?

BATH-SHEBA

The people, my son: They have been told that all of—

SOLOMON

To Satan with the people! Am I king to be ruled like a communal puppet? Must "Solomon" forever be a word for weakness in the mouths of foreign princes? Here is the smallest grant within chance of acceptance by Tyre! Only because of the people and their witless opinions have I drawn it so fine! The best advice counseled a grant many times as great! The *best* advice! And not that of any Jew! . . . Let me hear no more of the people. Where is the Phoenician?

AHISHER
(Who has entered and has been waiting)
Ahuram of Tyre, my lord!

(AHURAM *enters R. His face holds an angry welt raised by* TAHPNES' *whip.)*

AHURAM
(He goes to his knee)
My lord!

SOLOMON
Rise. (AHURAM *obeys.)*
I have considered King Hiram's demands. Israel would be pleased to pay her debts in gold or goods. At this time it is impossible—as your king well knows. I offer this. (*He passes the tablet*) Read it.

AHURAM
(He scans the grant)
My lord.

SOLOMON
The land is fertile and will be of value to Tyre—as

213

Tyrian good will is of value to Israel. I urge King Hiram to accept it as payment in full of Israel's debt—in the name of past regard, present wisdom and future peace. You will tell him so.

AHURAM

I shall, my lord.

SOLOMON

Farewell! May your gods be with you.

AHURAM

My lord! (*He bends his knee, exits R.*)

IDLER C

By Joshua, my lord, that was masterly!

IDLER A

He will certainly know he can take the land or a spot of war!

SOLOMON

Nothing of the kind: he is a fox. He knows what I think of casual war. But he is a kindly fox. At worst we will slice the debt and maintain our credit. (*The mob roar swells suddenly to new volume.*) What in Satan's *name?* Do I rule men or animals?

ZABUD

(*Peering between the curtains*)

It is the prophet Ahijah, my lord, and five workers, on the steps. They argue with the captain Boz.

214

SOLOMON

Pah! Let them argue! Close the curtains! (ZABUD *obeys.*) And do not call that charlatan a prophet! Black evil in the mind is not the mark of— (*The mob voice thunders.*) Great *heavens!* What *ails* the people? This grows beyond patience! Where is *Azariah?*

ZABUD

It is very strange, my lord.

SOLOMON

Strange, yes! (*To* ZADOK) And fatal, rabbi!—to your son's career!

ZADOK

My lord, it is not *like* my son to—to fail in duty.

ZABUD

Yes, my lord, I fear something is badly wrong.

SOLOMON

Wrong? How, where?

ZABUD

I don't know. But Jeroboam, Azariah—and the absence of Benaiah—

SOLOMON

You accuse Benaiah?

ZABUD

No, my lord!

215

MOTHER OF THAT WISDOM

SOLOMON

Then hold your tongue—or chance the losing of it.

BOZ

*(Snapping curtains apart he enters abruptly C,
descends steps, bends knee)*

My lord! A committee of five workers!—they demand audience with the king!

SOLOMON

Demand! Do they, now! How interesting! And my
good friend Ahijah, what does he demand?

BOZ

Nothing, my lord. He made passage for the five
through the multitude.

SOLOMON

For his creatures. Of course. They demand, do they?
(*He feels grimly amused. He laughs*) Very well, usher
them in. (*And to his group—as* BOZ *ascends steps and
moves off through curtains*:) You see? Annoyance,
rubbed *in* and *through*, can come out as a giggle.

(THE MEN OF NAPHTALI, ISSACHAR, ZEBULON,
ASHER *and* SIMEON *are thrust through parted curtains.* BOZ *and two guards herd them down the
steps.*)

ASHERITE

(He stumbles)

Gently, you fancy dog!

MOTHER OF THAT WISDOM

BOZ

To your knees! (*He snaps his whip at their legs*)
To your knees!

NAPHTALITE

(*As the* TRIBESMEN *obey sketchily*)
May you choke on your lash, you bloated louse!

ASHERITE

Shiny swine!

ISSACHARITE

Reeking *vulture!*

ZEBULONITE

Tyrant!

BOZ

Silence! (*Lashing their legs. The two guards start
forward.*)

SOLOMON

Hold. (*Waving the guards back*). . . . A committee.
I am touched. Representing what?

TRIBESMEN (*All but* SIMEONITE)

The people!
The workers!
The tribes!
Galilee!

SOLOMON

Hush. One at a time. (*He indicates* ZEBULONITE)
Who are you?

217

MOTHER OF THAT WISDOM

ZEBULONITE

Enough to say that I am the voice of Zebulon!—and
Ephraim and Manasseh!

NAPHTALITE

And I of Naphtali and Dan!

ISSACHARITE

And I of Issachar and Gad!

SIMEONITE
(Quietly)
And I of Simeon, Benjamin and Reuben.

ASHERITE

And I of *Asher!*—and the warning voice of the slaves
of Edom and Damascus!—

SOLOMON

Enough, enough! Voices. Lower your own or be
flogged.

ASHERITE
(To his fellows)
The whip, you see, the whip!

NAPHTALITE

Are you a Philistine that you think to frighten a Jew
with a bit of leather?

ASHERITE

We laugh at your whips! Ha, ha!

218

ISSACHARITE

We spit on whips and whippers! (*He spits.*)

ZEBULONITE

And on *tyrants!* (*He spits.*)

SOLOMON

Enough, I say! Silence!

ASHERITE

We did not come to be silent, we came to give warning!

ZADOK

Peace, peace, you cannot warn the king!

ASHERITE

What, are we slaves then?

NAPHTALITE

Is this Egypt? Does Pharaoh flog us to blind obedience?

ISSACHARITE

Then Moses and Joshua were dreams!—and it is of no moment to her tribes that Galilee is hacked from Canaan for the shameful debts of Judah!

SOLOMON
(*To* ZABUD)

What drivel is this?

219

MOTHER OF THAT WISDOM

NAPHTALITE

Drivel, he says!—that men of Naphtali should be Phoenician slaves!

ZABUD

No part of Naphtali is given to Tyre.

NAPHTALITE

Lies, lies! The thing is known!

ZABUD

What thing?

ISSACHARITE

Do not mock us! From the mouth of God's prophet we know you have ceded Galilee!

SOLOMON

"God's prophet!" Satan's liar!

ISSACHARITE

He impugns the word of the Holy Man!

SIMEONITE
(Quietly, as usual)
Do you deny that Galilee will be Tyre's?

ZABUD

Gently. A tiny and Phoenician-populated strip of the Galilean border has been offered as a—

MOTHER OF THAT WISDOM

ASHERITE
Lies, tricks!

ZEBULONITE
The Holy Man warned us!

ASHERITE
We are mocked!

SOLOMON
An end to this! You have had the truth! Believe what you will and go!

ZADOK
If you have further words for the king, say them quickly.

SIMEONITE
We lose by confusion, brothers. Let us speak as we planned.

ISSACHARITE
As we planned, yes!

NAPHTALITE
Yes! In order!

ASHERITE
Yes! Then I am first! So I say to the king: he shall call it *wicked* that Galilee be separated from Israel!

MOTHER OF THAT WISDOM

NAPHTALITE

And he shall call it *wicked* that Israel be burdened with new taxes!

ZEBULONITE

And he shall call *wicked* the further drafting of men out of Israel for labor in godless Judah!

NAPHTALITE

Even now the tribes go hungry for lack of men to grow sufficient food!

SIMEONITE

Hush! That is not as we planned.

NAPHTALITE

Hush me not! I say what should be said!

ISSACHARITE

You are out of turn! *My* words come next!

SIMEONITE

Yes, yes. Say them.

ISSACHARITE

(*To* NAPHTALITE)

Dolt! (*To* SOLOMON) And I of Issachar say: The king shall call *obscenely* wicked the building of temples to false and filthy gods!

SOLOMON

Pah! You bore me! Go, get out!

222

MOTHER OF THAT WISDOM

ALL *but* SIMEONITE
(They howl)

No, no! We have not finished!
We have *more* to say!
The ultimatum!
Yes, the ultimatum!
We must speak the ultimatum!

SIMEONITE

Peace! Peace, *hold!* Let me *speak!* (*The four quiet.*)
Confusion, always confusion.

(He approaches SOLOMON, *introducing a note of general quiet. He is almost confidential)* Shall I tell King
Solomon exactly how it is with the people out there?

SOLOMON

(In mocking imitation of the confidential attitude)
Tell King Solomon exactly.

SIMEONITE

It is thus: They wait for our return. The prophet
Ahijah stands among them watching the shadow of his
staff. The shadow strikes a mark. We have not returned
with word of hope. He cries out. The people rise and
destroy Jerusalem.

SOLOMON

Really? Sweeping aside the City Host?

SIMEONITE

There is no City Host. The captains lie entranced and
the soldiers mingle with the people.

223

SOLOMON
Why, how grim. And the Northern Host?

SIMEONITE
Benaiah supports the new king.

SOLOMON
What? We have a new king? Let me guess. Jeroboam!

SIMEONITE
His name has been spoken.

SOLOMON
Astonishing! Well, I *am* in a keg of brine. What would you suggest?

SIMEONITE
The people suggest, my lord. Nay, the people command:—that the king appear now at the Place of Judgment and publicly declare his hatred of the wickedness we have detailed!

SOLOMON
The people command. The king replies: He will first see them dancing on the red coals of hell!

(The other TRIBESMEN *howl.)*

TRIBESMEN
Vah! Vah!
Woe to the tongue that said it!

He curses the people!
Woe and doom to an unholy house!
God turn the curse against him!

NAPHTALITE
(Thrusting close to SOLOMON*)*
How *fitting* from a king who weds an Egyptian *whore!*

*(*SOLOMON *strikes the* NAPHTALITE *on the head with the butt of a whip.* NAPHTALITE *sinks to his knees.* ASHERITE, ISSACHARITE *and* ZEBULONITE *draw knives to attack* SOLOMON. SIMEONITE *steps back. The* FOUR IDLERS *seize the attackers from behind, hold them. . . . guards seize all the* TRIBESMEN.*)*

SOLOMON
Remove their tongues and eyes and hang them by their necks on the site of the temple of Ra!

(The four attacking TRIBESMEN, *struggling and shouting, are dragged R and off. The* SIMEONITE, *nearing exit R, jerks free of his guard, races up the steps, tears open the curtains.)*

SIMEONITE
(He screams)
Rise! The king has cursed the people!

(He leaps from the Place of Judgment as the guard takes after him. The mob roar begins.)

225

MOTHER OF THAT WISDOM

AHIJAH

(Off)

Rise! Rise! Ruin and death in the name of Jehovah!

(The mob roar swells, now holding a vicious note.)

SOLOMON

The storm curtains! Lower them! (*The outside curtains of tan wool are lowered. The noise of the mob is deadened*) Zabud! I want the City Host turned loose in full force!

ZABUD

My lord, the messengers have not returned!

SOLOMON

Then do we sit here like brainless women? Do something!

ZADOK

My lord, we must face possibilities. On all sides we hear that the soldiers mingle with the people.

SOLOMON

You believe those madmen? That scores of captains are faithless? Including your son?

ZADOK

No, my lord, but—perhaps a plot—

SOLOMON

Plot my royal arse! Your stupid son sits waiting for orders! Very well, get them to him!—

SERVANT

(He enters hastily R)

My lord, the lord Zadok's messenger!

(A breathless MESSENGER *enters, goes to knee.)*

SOLOMON

Well? Speak!

MESSENGER

My lord, I have seen a strange thing! The captains of the City Host lie entranced!

SOLOMON

Entranced? You mean, drunk?

MESSENGER

No, my lord, they lie as in death, breathing but staring, their eye points drawn small to near nothing! The people walk among them marveling!

SOLOMON

And the soldiers?

MESSENGER

There is none in the barracks, my lord!

ZADOK

The captain Azariah?

MESSENGER

He too sleeps, my lord!

227

MOTHER OF THAT WISDOM

SOLOMON
(Seizing the man by his robe front)
If you are lying, you creature—!

BATH-SHEBA
*(Throughout the working of events as she has foreseen
them she has sat in quiet observation)*
Why should he lie, my son? And why should God's
power cause wonder?—God, who drowned the hordes
of Egypt.

(Only SOLOMON'S *head does not bend.)*

SOLOMON
. . . God. . . . Well, God or Jeroboam, the crown is
not off balance! Arm the servants, the slaves, arm every
man in the palace! (*To his personal guards*) Out on the
steps, you four! And send in the captain Boz! (*As the
guards part the curtains in exit a fury of sound comes
in.*)
Zabud! Send word by swift horse to Benaiah, in
Megiddo! I want the chariot army! He will speed it,
speed it!—

AHISHER
(Striving to master agitation he enters R)
My lord! (*On his knee*) The captain of the Southern
Host is here!

SOLOMON
Shimei?

AHISHER

He, my lord! My lord, he bids me warn that he brings news that is evil!

SOLOMON

Is there news that is not evil? (*He shouts*) Come in, man, come in!

(He enters R. He is travel-stained. A worker's robe covers his uniform. Under the robe he holds his helmet; it carries the blue plume of the Southern Host.)

SHIMEI

(He tosses off the robe, goes to his knee)
My lord!

SOLOMON

Shimei, welcome! Speak!

SHIMEI

(He keeps to his knee)

I have sped from the Hebron garrison, my lord. The lord Jeroboam tarries there. He goes about boasting like a meat-bloated lion that the king has fallen and the throne is his through fulfillment of a prophecy by Ahijah. He commanded me to serve him, saying the full host was his through the support of Benaiah.

SOLOMON

Pah! Fallen, have I? Benaiah serve a jackal? *Pah!* Rise!

MOTHER OF THAT WISDOM

SHIMEI

My lord! (*He keeps to his knee;* AHISHER *also*) At dawn chariots drove through Hebron—and the man whom I knew as Ad'hotep the Egyptian.

SOLOMON

The queen Tahpnes' man?

SHIMEI

He, my lord. He declared himself to be Hadad, a prince of Edom. He journeyed to Edom to lead hordes against Israel.

SOLOMON

What sort of madness is this? You seized the fool?

SHIMEI

He was not alone, my lord. There was a great one with him. One who mocked the king, who spat upon Israel and cursed Jehovah!

SOLOMON

. . . Benaiah?

AHISHER

(*Since* SHIMEI *does not speak*)
. . . My lord!

SOLOMON

Speak!

230

MOTHER OF THAT WISDOM

SHIMEI

The queen Tahpnes, my lord. (SOLOMON *seizes* SHIMEI *by the throat.*)

AHISHER

My lord, no! He says the truth! The queen's pavilion is abandoned!

ZADOK
(As SHIMEI *chokes)*
In the name of God, my lord, cease! (*Grasping* SOLOMON'*s wrist.*)

AHISHER

My lord, we found this tablet! From the queen! See! Here! (SOLOMON *relaxes his hold*) Directed to you and closed with the queen's name! (SOLOMON *releases an uncomfortable* SHIMEI, *straightens, takes the tablet.*)

(*To* ZADOK, *as* SOLOMON *reads*) Foul, *foul!* (SOLOMON *drops the tablet. It shatters on the floor. Dull, drained, he moves to his chair-throne—sits.*)

BATH-SHEBA
(Close to him, her hand on his shoulder)
My son—

ZADOK

O great Jehovah! Give strength and stern comfort to the king of Israel!

ALL

Amen!

BATH-SHEBA

Oh, my son——

BOZ

(Battered and bleeding he enters C, the uproar of the
fighting mob blasting in momentarily as the curtains
part and close)
My lord! The steps cannot be held! The men tire!
If the king would flee he should do so now!

BATH-SHEBA

Flee?

ZADOK

My lord, he speaks wisely.

ZABUD

Yes, my lord!——through Benaiah's passage!

BATH-SHEBA
(To BOZ)
How long *can* you hold?

BOZ

Minutes, my lady, and not a score of them——without
swords.

BATH-SHEBA

Do your utmost——without swords.

232

MOTHER OF THAT WISDOM

BOZ

My lady. (*He turns, sees* SHIMEI) Shimei!

SHIMEI

Boz, old Hebrew!

BOZ

You are getting fat, old Hebrew! (*As they embrace rapidly*) Come work it off! (*Both exit C.*)

ZABUD

My lord, we should start immediately. . . . (SOLOMON *makes no response*) My lord!

BATH-SHEBA

Ahijah knows of the passage. Do you think he will not have it watched?

IDLER D

We should be glad to precede the king, my lady, and sort of clear the way.

IDLER A

Nothing like the shock of smart violence.

IDLER B

Tempered.

IDLER C

The *flat* of the sword, of *course*. (And to ZABUD— *since* BATH-SHEBA *has not been listening:*) You could use us, my lord?

233

ZABUD

Yes. Thank you. In a moment. (*To* SOLOMON) My lord. . . . My lord, there is no time to be lost.

SOLOMON

. . . Time?

ZABUD

You must rouse yourself. We must flee. . . . My lord!

SOLOMON

. . . Yes—yes—(*He rises—stands*) Yes.

BATH-SHEBA

. . . The king of Israel flees in cowardly panic.

ZABUD

My lady!—

BATH-SHEBA

The son of David runs like a frightened child from the fat shadow of a thin stick.

SOLOMON

. . . David fled before Absalom.

BATH-SHEBA

Before a true enemy—the better to turn and destroy him! You flee before no enemy, only a bewildered people and a poor sick-minded old rabbi.

MOTHER OF THAT WISDOM

SOLOMON

What would you have me do? Stay here and die? I should not mind particularly.

BATH-SHEBA

What a noble thing to say! The fate of God's own kingdom in your hands, the happiness or misery of a whole people, and you speak of suicide!

ZADOK

My lady—

BATH-SHEBA

Silence! . . . You ask, what would I have you do? I would have you do what you never yet have done: I would have you face yourself. I would have you count your misdeeds. I would have you think of the whips that have cut into the backs of proud Jews because they balked at rags and starvation! and persecution and slavery! while you wasted their substance! Would you call *yourself* a Jew if Jews would submit to the indignities you have put upon them? Are you an *utter* fool that you can not see merit in their fury? Alternately you have patronized them, ignored them and scorned them when your heart should have sung with pride that Jehovah gave you the leadership of such a race of men! What would I have you do? I would have you face your victims! Out there! Now! Not as king but as a brother Jew who grants the wrong he has done and humbly begs a chance to right it! . . . They may kill you. But if you do less than this then surely you are no seed of David, but Satan spat into my womb! . . .

*(*SOLOMON *is no longer dull. Quietly, but positively, his bearing and expression have changed. Now they suggest calm strength that is deeply real and solid. He exhibits neither trace of shame nor any lofty glow of picturesque enlightenment and reformation.)*

SOLOMON
(To BATH-SHEBA*)*
. . . I shall do that: face myself—and them. (*To* ZADOK) My crown.

(Jehoshaphat lifts the crown from its box. SOLOMON *kneels. All kneel.* ZADOK *removes the gold circlet from* SOLOMON'S *head, takes the crown, holds it up.)*

ZADOK
O great Jehovah, give now to Solomon such fortitude and wisdom as his supreme need requires! (*He lowers the crown to* SOLOMON'S *head. Then softly*) Jehovah— help him. Amen!

SOLOMON
(He rises. All rise)
Open the curtains.

MOTHER OF THAT WISDOM

(The curtains are opened wide. The noise of the struggling mob blasts in.

As SOLOMON *starts up the steps* BATH-SHEBA *goes to her knees;* ABISHAG *also. The four* IDLERS *draw their swords and crouch on the steps.*

SOLOMON *continues up and out of the Place of Judgment. He stands motionless, facing the people. At sight of him the roar of the mob swells to its greatest height. Stones fly past him, some fall into the pavilion.*

A stone strikes him in the temple. He reels, raises a hand to his head, touches blood. Straightening he lifts the crown from his head, holds it before him— not affectedly. The mob roar lessens.)

VOICES

Hear him! Hear the tyrant! Let him speak that we may mock his lies! Speak, tyrant! Speak before you die! **Speak!**

SOLOMON
(Strongly)

Fellow Jews!

VOICES

Yah! Yaaah! Fellow Jews, now! Now he is a Jew! Now he is one of us! You, a Jew? Yaaah! The Egyptian

237

lover, a Jew! Yaaaah! (SOLOMON *raises the crown, slightly, as though, unarrogantly, he asks to be heard*) Let him speak, let him speak! Hear him! Let him condemn himself! Yaah, out of his own mouth! Hear him! . . . (*The roar subsides.*)

SOLOMON

Yesterday you heard Ahijah the Shilonite say, "Let the king pass judgment upon himself!" (*A mocking reaction that spends itself shortly*) Today *I* say, let Solomon the *man* pass judgment upon the king of Israel!

VOICE OF AHIJAH

Lies, lies, tricks and lies! I, Ahijah, say, the guilty king is condemned!

VOICES

Yes, yes, tried and condemned! Away with him! Condemned! Away with the tyrant! No, no, hear and mock! Hear him! Let him condemn himself! Let him speak! . . .

SOLOMON

Solomon the man says of the king: The people hungered and went in rags! Out of their misery they cried to you for help! Rather than food and clothing you gave them taxes, taxes, and the lash! Therefore you merit *death!*

(*The mob is stunned to a moment of relative quiet.*)

238

AHIJAH

Trickery! Lies and trickery! Enough! Rise!

VOICES

Trickery! Lies! Pagan trickery! Vah! Away with the pagan! Hear him, hear him! Let him condemn himself! Let him speak! Hear him! . . .

SOLOMON

Solomon the man says of the king: You made a plan to drag your people from honest toil and drive them as slaves to the building of temples to false gods! You mocked the holy name of Jehovah by taking to wife a strange and vile woman of a hated foreign land! Therefore you too are vile and merit *death!*

(Again a hushed moment.)

VOICE OF AHIJAH

Men of Israel, in the name of Jehovah I warn you! The tongue of Solomon is a serpent to find your hearts with cunning poison!

VOICES

Poison, yes! Vaaah! A serpent! Peace, rabbi, peace! Let him speak! Let the people judge! Yes, yes, let the people judge!

A VOICE

Tell us! Does Solomon ask for death?

239

MOTHER OF THAT WISDOM

SOLOMON

Solomon declares that the king is death-worthy! Between the king and death there stands but one thing: the mercy of the men of Israel! You guards! Drop your whips! Drop them! . . . Now may there never again be seen a royal whip in Israel! (*And above a moan of wonder*) Guards! Withdraw! Completely! Go! . . . (*The helmets of several guards may be seen as they ascend palace steps and move off R and L*) Now may there never again be weapons of war between the throne and the people!

AHIJAH

(*Above a rising expression of rumbling wonder*)

You *fools,* I say to you woe, *woe* to Israel if you permit yourselves to be—

VOICES

Peace, rabbi, peace! Let him speak! Let us see this thing and hear it! Let the king speak!

SOLOMON

The king can speak now only as a brother Jew!—one who grants the wrongs he has done and begs a chance to right them!

A VOICE

Galilee, what of Galilee?

VOICES

Yes, Galilee! Galilee!

240

MOTHER OF THAT WISDOM

SOLOMON

Let the people decide! In north Galilee, in Asher, on
the very border of Phoenicia, lie three small towns: Hazrah, Taadish and Keda! The lands are poor, the popula-
tions, even now, nine-tenths Phoenician! Shall Israel
bargain with Tyre? Tyre to cancel outright the enormous
debt of Israel? Tyre to receive in return this worthless
morsel of land? Let the people decide!

VOICES

Yes! Yes! A bargain! The debt for the towns! The
towns for old Hiram, a clean slate for us! Yes! Yes! A
deal! Out-fox old Hiram-the-fox! (*There is laughter
among the voices.*)

SOLOMON

The king will do the will of the people! In this and
all things! (*He raises his head skyward*) O great Jehovah, the king renounces wickedness! The wickedness of
taxation that is unjust! The wickedness of labor drafts
that burden men beyond need and reason! And above
all, such wickedness as led him to take to his bosom a
heathen *whore!*—that woman of Egypt whose feet, by
Thy mercy, no longer befoul the sacred soil of Israel!
O great Jehovah, show mercy to the king and give him
strength! . . . (*To the people*) These are the words of
the king! These are his determinations, these things he
covenants! And if he does less, then surely he is no son
of David, *but Satan spat into his mother's womb!* (He
lowers his head.)

241

MOTHER OF THAT WISDOM

*(The people respond with a sustained roar of appro-
bation. Prompted by* BATH-SHEBA, ZADOK *ascends
steps to* SOLOMON's *side. He takes the crown from*
SOLOMON's *hands, holds it up toward the people.)*

VOICES

Yes! Give him the crown! Yes! Crown him! Crown
the son of David! Yes, let him right his wrongs! Crown
him!

*(*SOLOMON *kneels before* ZADOK.*)*

ZADOK

Almighty God, give wisdom to the son of David, that
he may know himself at all times! Let his ears be healthy
and his eyes sharp that he may hear and see the needs
of his people! Let his heart hold worthiness and mercy
that he may fill the needs of his people, to each man
more than his merited measure; that he may take for
himself less, always less than his royal opportunity will
permit! Great Jehovah, bless the king of Israel! Amen!

THE PEOPLE

Amen!

*(*ZADOK *crowns* SOLOMON. *To the approving voice
of the people,* SOLOMON *rises, faces them—as*
ZADOK *steps back and descends to the pavilion,*
AHIJAH *charges up the palace steps to the Place
of Judgment, faces the people.)*

AHIJAH

Tricks and infamy! In the name of the one God and

242

as the mouth of the one God I say, *a curse on this infamy!* By Jehovah's flaming word the House of David *dies* and *Jeroboam* sits upon the throne of Israel—

(The rising voice of the people drowns out AHIJAH's *words. He stands, a figure of mad and terrible frustration. Abruptly he wheels, drawing his sword. To the voiced horror of the people and the group on stage proper, he raises it to bring it down on* SOLOMON's *head. . . . But he stiffens, the sword falls and he collapses before* SOLOMON *in a convulsive seizure. The people react as at the sight of a miracle of God.)*

SOLOMON
(He calls down to ZABUD*)*
Wine and water!

(He goes to a knee beside AHIJAH, *wipes his mouth with a kerchief.)* ZABUD *ascends steps with wine and water and* SOLOMON *ministers to* AHIJAH. . . . *As* AHIJAH *stirs two followers ascend palace steps to him. He rises. Bowed and stumbling he exits down the steps supported by the followers. Again* SOLOMON *faces the people. Their frenzied acclamation completes his triumph. He turns and descends to the pavilion. From here the crowd noises rapidly diminish to silence as the multitude disperses. Fervidly and with bent knee* SOLOMON *is greeted by all on stage—except* ZADOK *and* ZABUD *who stand and beam fondly, and* BATH-SHEBA *who weeps and embraces him.)*

243

MOTHER OF THAT WISDOM

BATH-SHEBA
My son, *oh,* my son!

SOLOMON
My mother.

VARIOUS ONES
My lord, no day ever was as great as this!
Not ever! The king is the greatest of all kings!
Now surely the king will reign forever!
My lord, this triumph will never be forgotten!

IDLER A
My lord, we think you must be the wisest man that ever lived!

SOLOMON
Thank you, I remind myself of the ass that was lost in a field of corn. He, too, was wise. He ate corn.

(*Laughter.* SOLOMON *kneels before* ZADOK. *All* **kneel.**)

ZADOK
Jehovah preserve the king of Israel! (*He removes the crown from* SOLOMON's *head, replaces it with the gold circlet*) Jehovah bless you, my son! Amen!

SOLOMON
(He rises. All rise)
Zabud, there are posts to be filled. Consult with me regarding these young men. I owe my life to them.

244

MOTHER OF THAT WISDOM

FOUR IDLERS

Thank you, my lord! My lord, thank you!—

(BOZ and SHIMEI enter C, descend steps.)

SOLOMON

Shimei, Boz, look into this odd collapse of the host captains. I suspect Ahijah and Jeroboam, and the use of some sort of drug.

BATH-SHEBA

Oh, hardly, my son! *Scores* of captains? It is really a classic case of summer food poisoning.

SOLOMON

. . . Perhaps. Oh, and Boz: release those four tribesmen. Zabud, speak to them, and to the one that escaped. If possible, appoint them as salaried intermediaries— with staves of office. Immediately.

ZABUD, BOZ and SHIMEI

My lord! (*They bend a knee and exit R.*)

ITTAI

(He enters R running, goes to his knee. He carries the two halves of a broken clay tablet)

My lord!

SOLOMON

Ittai! Where have *you* been?

ITTAI

Locked out, my lord. The palace gates were barred.

MOTHER OF THAT WISDOM

BATH-SHEBA

I sent him to inqure regarding the inactivity of the host.

ITTAI

I found the captain Azariah collapsed over a pot of crawling food, my lord.

SOLOMON

Crawling?

BATH-SHEBA

There, I knew it! Food poisoning!

ITTAI

He fell with this in his hand, my lord. (*He hands* SOLOMON *the broken tablet. As* SOLOMON *reads the tablet* ITTAI *turns to* BATH-SHEBA, *murmurs*) My lady—(*He slips her* KINYRAS's *jeweled drug dispenser.*)

BATH-SHEBA
(*Murmuring, concealing the casket*)
Thank you, Ittai.

SOLOMON

From Benaiah! Explaining his absence, pledging his allegiance!

BATH-SHEBA

There now! Of course! One should never listen to rumors.

MOTHER OF THAT WISDOM

ZADOK

Praise Jehovah!

SOLOMON

Yes, praise Him—and Satan take all scandal mongers. And now I thank all of you for your loyalty. I am very weary. Leave me, taking with you my blessing and the gratitude of Israel.

(*All but* BATH-SHEBA, ABISHAG *and* ITTAI *exit appropriately.* SOLOMON *stretches out on his divan, sighs, explores his injured temple with his fingers*) I am a battered king.

BATH-SHEBA

Oh, your poor head!—I had forgotten! Here, let me see. (*She kneels L beside his divan, removes the circlet from his head*) Why, it is really *cut!* Abishag: wine, water and a cloth. Outrageous. It should be against the laws of Israel to throw anything but *round* stones. Hurry, dear.

(ABISHAG *obeys. She has been intimately near* ITTAI *who sits U, noiselessly tuning his lute.*)

SOLOMON

A position for one of those young men: Royal Examiner of Stones to Be Thrown at the King.

(ABISHAG, *delivering wound aids, kneels R beside* SOLOMON.)

BATH-SHEBA

Hush. (*Bathing his wound*) No one ever again will throw a stone at my son. Lean your head.

SOLOMON

(He sighs contentedly)

How sweet is the comfort of Afterward, when *Before* held the *itch* of the End. . . . No— (*Wrinkling his nose*) that is perhaps not very excellently said.

BATH-SHEBA

"Itch" indeed. Scurfy.

SOLOMON

Yes. Ittai, sing for me. A wordless song.

(REHOBOAM *enters, running, draws up panting, wide-eyed.*)

REHOBOAM

My father! The queen! They say she has gone! Tell me it is not true!

SOLOMON

The daughter of the pharaoh has returned to Egypt.

REHOBOAM

She is—coming back?

SOLOMON

Not while I live.

248

REHOBOAM
(He backs)
. . . You drove her away!

BATH-SHEBA
Rehoboam—

REHOBOAM
I loved her and you drove her away!

SOLOMON
My son.

REHOBOAM
No! *No! Not* your son! You are a—a *Semitic beast!*
(Sobbing hysterically he darts from the stage.)

SOLOMON
(He jumps to his feet)
By the Almighty, I will—

BATH-SHEBA
No, No! *Enough!* That is not the way! . . . (SOLOMON
is held) The child is not responsible. The woman molded
him. Even you were lost. (SOLOMON *drops his head*) Sit,
my son—recline. . . . (SOLOMON *obeys. She bathes his
wound*) He has been walking in strange and dangerous
ways. He has come to a place of hideous confusion. You
must give him *your* hand now—and lead him—remembering that you lead a king, and the fate of Israel itself.

SOLOMON

. . . Oh, Mama! I am such a stupid man!

BATH-SHEBA

No—not stupid. You have done stupid things. All men do. It is their way of learning wisdom.

SOLOMON

Jehovah speed the process.

BATH-SHEBA

He will. Already men *think* you are wise.

(ITTAI *has been striking his lute lightly. Close to* SOLOMON *he begins to hum softly.*)

SOLOMON
(He smiles)

The little mama. (*He pats her cheek*) I am very fortunate. (*He turns a mite on his divan*) And the little Abishag. (*He pats* her *cheek*) . . . But not so little any more! (*He fondles her arm, his eyes observing her ample bosom as she kneels beside him, head down*) Not little at all! See, Mama, our baby Shunamite has grown quite—up.

BATH-SHEBA

Turn your head till I use the wine.

SOLOMON

No, it is comfortable now. (*He leans nearer to* ABI-

250

SHAG) My dear, it is surprising. You have bloomed! (ITTAI *ceases to strum and hum—and rasps his lute— drawing* SOLOMON's *fleeting but knowing attention.*) Quite bloomed! Did you do it just lately?

BATH-SHEBA

My *son,* your wound needs further attention.

SOLOMON

Peace, Mama. This is a wonderful thing. She is a woman. See, Ittai! Yesterday a child, today a woman! Are *all* men blind? (*Closer to* ABISHAG, *he laughs to himself with tongue in cheek*) My dove, I *have* been blind and neglectful. I have caused you to suffer. I know, I know, by night on your bed you sought me and found me not. Can you forgive me?

ABISHAG

No! Yes!

(ITTAI *whangs his lute discordantly.*)

BATH-SHEBA

My son!

SOLOMON

My dove, my lovely dove, I know you do. Given legs for it I shall come to you tonight, I promise. As soon as it is dark. You will be my lily, my rose of Sharon. I shall be as free as a roe, as a young hart upon the mountains—

251

MOTHER OF THAT WISDOM

BATH-SHEBA

Solomon, what nonsense is this? Lilies, roes and harts. You sound like one of Ittai's songs. You must not tease your sister Abishag.

SOLOMON

How little you understand love, my mother. I was blind and now I see. (*He beams on* ITTAI, *then on* ABISHAG) She is full-fit for spousehood!

BATH-SHEBA

You are not really serious?

SOLOMON

I am very serious. I speak of love. Love is a serious thing. And a good thing. Good, do you hear? . . . (*Momentarily sincere*) That frightful woman is gone! Out of Israel and out of me! . . . (*Then tongue again in cheek*) And now I see the delightful posibilities of true love in this lovely— (*He gestures*) Abishag! Is that not a good thing?

BATH-SHEBA

Well, yes, but—tonight! It is not seemly! At least wait until—until it is more seemly!

SOLOMON

Oh, Mama, the poor child already has waited for years! (*He takes* ABISHAG's *hand, beaming on* ITTAI) Sing, Ittai—of love. (ITTAI *passes a leaden hand across the lute strings, sings wordlessly and almost gruntingly in a key and fashion that are very low— as* BATH-SHEBA

252

draws KINYRAS'*s drug casket from a waist pocket, fingers it, peeks at it—the while* SOLOMON *is murmuring against the horrified ear of* ABISHAG:) Oh, my dove, my lily, you will be a lovely rose!—tonight, tonight! And I shall be the ghost of that roe, that young hart upon the mountains—

BATH-SHEBA

Well! (*Abruptly smiling*) If you are really serious then this is a bridal festival! You must pledge each other with a cup of this full-drained wine! (*Filling two cups with wine*) A really significant occasion!

(SOLOMON *is seemingly preoccupied with the shut-eyed fondling of his lily-rose, but* ABISHAG *and* ITTAI *watch pop-eyed as* BATH-SHEBA operates the drug dispenser over one cup—*thus missing* SOLOMON'*s sly glance toward his mother's preoccupation*) There! . . . (*She gives* SOLOMON *the drugged wine,* ABISHAG *the other cup*) Drink, my children! For love *is* a good thing! Oh, *such* a good thing! Drink!

SOLOMON
(*He eyes the cup, sniffs it, murmurs*)
"Full-drained." . . . Ah, well! I do need a goodly spell of "full-drained" relaxation! (*He drinks.*)

ITTAI
(*He slaps a hearty chord on his lute and sings robustly*)
Behoooooold, thou art fair, my love! Behold, thou art fair! Thou hast dove's eyes!—

Curtain

253